Shrub Roses for Every Garden

For Heather
with all my love
from
Geoffrey
Christmas, 1974.

Michael Gibson

SHRUB ROSES FOR EVERY GARDEN

Illustrated by Marjorie Blamey

COLLINS
ST JAMES'S PLACE, LONDON

William Collins Sons & Co Ltd
London · Glasgow · Sydney · Auckland
Toronto · Johannesburg

First published 1973
© Michael Gibson 1973
ISBN 0 00 214070 5
Made and Printed in Great Britain by
William Collins Sons & Co Ltd Glasgow

Contents

List of Illustrations

Foreword

by R. C. Balfour

President, Royal National Rose Society

Although there are already some excellent books on shrub roses, a new one on the subject is most welcome at a time when gardeners are taking a much greater interest in shrub roses, both old and modern. Like its title this is an encouraging book, written by an experienced rosarian who grows over 200 varieties of roses in his Surrey garden and is a successful exhibitor as well as specialising in shrub roses. His aim is to encourage readers to grow shrub roses, whatever the size of their gardens, and to help them to choose those which will suit their particular conditions and climate and to use their talent to design a garden to suit their own taste and the time they can devote to its planting and maintenance. Although he mainly concentrates on the older shrub roses, he includes some modern varieties and climbing and pillar roses.

In his descriptions of each variety he gives useful advice about their special qualities or needs and suggests some unusual ways of growing them. He also mentions a number of other plants which, as I too have found, blend or contrast well with roses.

The book is delightfully illustrated by Marjorie Blamey whose beautiful watercolour paintings should be a great help in identifying the older roses as well as giving much pleasure in themselves.

I commend this book to all who love roses at home or overseas and enjoy reading about them.

CHAPTER I

Why Shrub Roses?

WHAT is a shrub rose? How is it different from other roses?

Basically, of course, all roses are shrubs. *The Concise Oxford Dictionary* defines a shrub as a "Woody plant of less size than a tree and usually divided into separate stems from near the ground." Well, that certainly covers all roses, so where are we? Apparently in the position of the man whose wife said to him, "How typical of you to side with the dictionary against me."

But the dictionary is right, of course, and the term shrub roses is an artificial one, used broadly to cover those roses which are not, like the usual run of Hybrid Teas (HTs) and floribundas, used for bedding. They do cover some of the larger HTs and floribundas which are big enough to make specimen bushes on their own and are too tall for massing in the average bed, and some of the less vigorous climbers when these are grown without the support of a wall or trellis – as shrubs, in other words – but in the main it is used for roses that were popular in Victorian times and earlier (often known as Old Fashioned or Old Roses), for species, and for certain modern varieties which have been bred to resemble them.

A great many enthusiasts for shrub roses praise them to the skies, overdoing it, I feel, in their enthusiasm and sometimes causing disappointment for those who are trying them out for the first time. At the same time they run down modern HTs and floribundas as if they were in some way greatly inferior. Of course they are not; they are different. In some respects some of them are better. In some respects others are worse. It is like running down a *Viburnum tomentosum mariesii* because it is not a Guelder Rose. Both are of the same genus, but once again they are different, though shrub roses do have one thing that gives them an exclusive appeal to many; they are not as yet widely enough grown to be common in gardens, and human nature being what it is . . .

To some people shrub roses are those old flowers with weird names, painted on table mats by that Frenchman – what was he called? Something from history, like the dodo. They are certainly from history – much of it fascinating – but they are very much alive and some of the best garden shrubs there are. No, I am not in my turn getting carried away. Consider my reasons for saying this.

Shrub roses come in all sizes, from about two feet tall to twelve or fifteen feet. They can be used as handsome specimens on their own, in mixed plantings with others of their kind or with other shrubs, and some of them will mix quite happily with non-shrubby border plants. They can be spreading and sprawling, bushy, or erect and upright. Some can be used as ground-cover, and others make effective sea-side shrubs, quite proof against the salt-laden air. Some can be used quite successfully for bedding if suitably pruned and the Hybrid Musk group in particular will outflower most floribundas if grown in this way. A few give rich autumn colouring with their leaves (the Rugosa group and two American species *Rosa foliolosa* and particularly *Rosa virginiana* with its crimson and later yellow and flame tints) while others have fragrant foliage. All have beautiful, and some really sumptuous flowers, in most cases scented, which are often followed by decorative heps in the autumn, resembling in shape, if not quite the size of, smooth-sided Coca-Cola bottles. They can be used for hedges, short and tall, semi-formal and informal; they can form great fountains of blossom climbing through trees.

A number of shrub roses have great historic interest and one can trace the development of our modern roses through them if one wants to. An old Persian wild rose, for instance, was responsible for all our yellow, orange and flame colours and not so long ago at that, and roses that had been cultivated in China for hundreds if not thousands of years, when crossed with ones from Europe gave us plants that would bloom right through to the autumn instead of just during June and July. The York and Lancaster rose of the Wars of the Roses, Shakespeare's Musk Rose and eglantine, the roses you see painted by the Dutch old masters – these are just a few.

Some shrub roses are so unusual in appearance that they can

form a point of special interest in your garden, which is always a nice thing to have. The green rose is one, and the many striped roses, roses with their petals fringed at the edges like pinks, and roses with the really spectacular heps that I mentioned just now.

The flowers themselves are mostly very different from the modern varieties. Many, especially of the species, are single, with a delicate beauty all their own and a profusion of bloom which is a revelation. Others are huge and globular with masses of petals, often opening flat with the petals folded and arranged in such a way that they divide the bloom into four or more sections, known as quartering. Others are loose and informal. It is only fairly recent fashion that has decreed that the perfect rose should have the high, pointed centre of the modern Hybrid Tea.

The colourings of the old roses are mostly soft pinks, mauves, creams and whites, though there are a few very dark purples and maroons. It was only as recently as 1900 that a French nursery-man named Pernet-Ducher produced the first really bright yellow rose in the modern idiom, using the Persian yellow wild rose I mentioned earlier as a parent.

These then are some of the attributes of a shrub rose that earn a plus mark. What about the other side?

Those who approach a Latin name like a dog approaching a hedgehog will already have had a warning from the short amount I have written so far. Three or four Latin names in the first few pages – this is not the book for me. There really is not much I can say by way of comfort. There is worse to come. A number of the roses have Latin names and several other names as well, which is I suppose inevitable with plants that have been growing for hundreds of years in different countries. Many of the old roses were raised in France, particularly after the time of Empress Josephine, who made roses fashionable garden flowers by forming a unique collection of all the species and varieties that were then available, at her home at Malmaison, outside Paris. Not surprisingly they have French names and some of them are quite terrifying to attempt to say, let alone spell. But this is, I am afraid, something that you will have to face up to, as all old rose lovers have to do in the beginning. I did, and look at what I have got myself into.

The worst speller in the world, and another seventeen chapters to write.

On the other hand some of the names are extremely beautiful and romantic, as old-fashioned as their owners. If you choose only these ones, you will still have a worthwhile collection and, while one rose may have several names now, at least you do not have to face the problem that buyers had at the time when Hybrid Perpetual roses were being superseded by HTs. Then there were two roses called Mme Eugène Verdier, an HP and an HT, an HT called Souvenir de Mme Eugène Verdier, an HP called Mademoiselle Eugène Verdier, a Mme Victor Verdier and a Victor Verdier. Things can always be more complicated and unless you are really going to start a big collection there is not so very much to learn.

A large number of shrub roses flower only once, in June and July. True, but most other shrubs flower only once and not many of them give such a spectacular display of bloom during their three or four weeks of glory as the best of the shrub roses. A number of shrub roses are described in catalogues as being repeat-flowering or recurrent. Many truly are, but there are also plenty so described that really have very little to say for themselves after the summer flush is over. Later on I will indicate which these are, but this does not mean that you should not grow them. Treat them as once-flowering shrubs that may give a bonus and you will not be disappointed. Most of the modern shrub roses now being bred do really flower more or less continuously, or at least have a very good repeat, but any rose of whatever kind must have its heps removed after the first flowering if it is to bloom well again. Shrub roses are no exception – just a little more difficult if they are ten feet tall.

Shrub roses need no pruning. How often has this been said and gladdened the hearts of those who approach a rose for pruning like Henry James approaching Mrs Pankhurst? To an extent it is true, in that most of them will continue to put on a good show for many years with little or no attention, other than the removal now and again of old, dead wood. But even this is not always as easy as it sounds. Many of the shrub roses are incredibly prickly and thorny and with the larger more bushy or sprawling growers, getting out old wood can be like

participating in a cat-fight. The thorns can make training haz-
ardous, too. If you want to get your own back on a slug, put it
at the top of a Rugosa or Scotch Rose bush with a lettuce on the
ground underneath.

But though many shrub roses do quite well without pruning,
almost without exception they will be a great deal better with
some regular attention, apart from the fact that you may well
have to keep the more wayward growers within bounds if your
space is limited, by reasonably frequent cutting back of the longer
shoots. The natural way for a rose to grow is to replace its old
and failing wood with new growth from the base or near it.
Pruning will allow this new growth room to develop properly
and will in fact encourage it to come more quickly. On most roses
it is the new shoots that bear the best flowers.

With certain notable exceptions – some of the species and most
of the Rugosa group of roses, for instance – mildew and/or black
spot and greenfly, and occasionally rust, can be just as active on
shrub roses as on any others. Hybrid Perpetuals, Bourbon Roses,
Gallica Roses and Damasks can all get mildew if the circumstances
are right for it, and the Persian yellow species is one of the worst
of all for black spot. Fortunately, however, most of the old roses
are so tough that they can shrug off attacks without apparent
harm to their constitutions, but this does not mean that you
should never spray them when diseases or pests appear. It will,
if nothing else, keep the bushes from looking unsightly.

Which brings me naturally to the fact that not all shrub roses
are things of great beauty when out of flower. Some do have
wonderful foliage, light and ferny, like Canarybird and some of
the Moyesii family hybrids. Some have beautiful rich green leaves
like the Rugosas. But it must be said that others do have dull,
uninteresting leaves, and if this is combined with gawky growth
as it is with the Centifolia roses, steps are needed to get over the
problem, for the Centifolia flowers are not to be missed. Careful
positioning when planting, which is dealt with in Chapter 3, can
solve a lot of the difficulties.

Again not all shrub roses are rain proof and some can look a
sorry sight after a day's downpour. That lovely white rose, Blanc
Double de Coubert, can look as if it were draped with small, wet

Kleenex after a heavy shower, but as with most of the others, new flowers follow so quickly that it does not matter too much.

Although the old roses are tough and in many cases will thrive almost anywhere provided they have sun, a number do need good cultivation and rich soil to give of their best. Otherwise their growth may be spindly and the flowers far below what they should be in quantity, size and intensity of colours. Good and thorough preparation of the bed before planting and an annual mulch of manure or compost will keep most of them very happy unless your soil is exceptionally poor.

By now you should have some idea of the best and the worst. To those who have seen the best, at its best, there can be no shadow of doubt which way the scales will tip, but a question very much to the point is: Why, if they are so wonderful, did the old roses go out of fashion? And why are they now coming back again into favour? Take the first point first.

Mr Pernet-Ducher must take a lot of the blame. The Chinese the rest. Pernet-Ducher introduced his revolutionary yellow rose,

PLATE I

Species and their hybrids   page

1. Canarybird   64
2. *cantabrigiensis*   65
3. *complicata*   65
4. *dupontii*   66
5. *ecae*   65
6. *foetida bicolor*   66
7. *foetida persiana*   67
8. *forrestiana*   67

Soleil d'Or in 1900, not long after the perpetual-flowering influence of the China roses was beginning to be felt. Tea roses with their China rose ancestry were being crossed day and night with every Hybrid Perpetual the raisers could lay their hands on to produce the exciting, more or less continuous-flowering, large-bloomed HTs. With startling new colours available as well as strong yellows and orange, the HT, such is the appeal of novelty, swept, as they say, all before it. The queues at the nurseries were miles long. Nurserymen bought yachts. The old was forgotten, or nearly so.

Not a great many people realise what comparative newcomers the HTs and floribundas are to the rose scene. HTs only really began to become popular after the 1914–18 war and floribundas after the last war. A list of roses "worth growing in this country" prepared by *Amateur Gardening* in 1899 gives a total of 2128 varieties in all. The list contains a lot of Bourbon roses, species, Gallica roses, China roses and other early kinds, but there are no fewer than 826 Hybrid Perpetuals named, not far off half of the

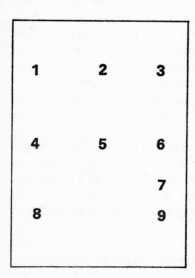

PLATE 2

Species and their hybrids   *page*

total. Against this there are only 140 HTs. Nowadays, just over seventy years later, there are probably not more than about a dozen Hybrid Perpetuals that you can buy without a considerable search (though a good many more are still growing in old gardens) and the total of HTs runs into thousands.

In the 1899 list there are still 540 varieties of Tea Rose listed. This was the kind of rose which, when crossed with the Hybrid Perpetuals, produced the first Hybrid Teas, and I suppose that at one time there must have been many more of them, though I do not know the peak total. However, considering that they are not really hardy in this country, even 540 varieties is a good figure. There must have been a large part of the United Kingdom under glass or else it was a question of fighting one's way through Tea Roses to get into Devon.

An interesting sidelight on the list is the number of roses of all kinds that were named after royalty or at least members of the nobility – something approaching 300 of them. There are Barons, Baronesses and Baronnes, Emperors and Empresses, Kaisers and Kaiserins, Königs and Königins, Lords and Ladies, Marquis, Présidents, Vicomtesses and Viscontes, and even a Sultan. Ducs, Duchesses, Dukes and Duchesses, Grand Ducs and Grande Duchesses come off second best with fifty varieties, while top of the tree with fifty-seven are Princesses. Strangely enough, disregarding foreign royalty, there is only one straight Queen – Victoria – unless you count names like Queen of the Bedders, and it would be lacking in respect to suggest who that might have been.

Gallic gallantry is very much in evidence with the names of 367 roses prefixed by Madame, and I am sure it was only the lack of female rose breeders that restricted the Monsieurs to fourteen. There can, however, be no excuse at all for there being only twenty-three Mrs roses from this country, and the single Mr is quite indefensible.

However, I seem to have got rather a long way from the reasons for the decline and present revival in the popularity of the shrub rose.

The facts do not seem to indicate that their often formidable names had anything to do with their decline, but I certainly think that they have handicapped their revival. As I said earlier, some of them are beautiful and romantic, but even so they take a bit of learning. What rose name today can beat for appeal Belle Amour, Great Maiden's Blush, Cardinal de Richelieu, Tricolore de Flandre, Tuscany Superb, Chapeau de Napoleon, Robert le Diable, Tour de Malakoff, Nuits de Young, Commandant Beaurepaire, Prince Camille de Rohan and Reine des Violettes? Who, on the other hand, would willingly face calling at his local nursery and asking for *Rosa cantabrigiensis*, *Rosa multibracteata*, *Rosa sericea pteracantha*, *Rosa spinosissima*, Roseraie de l'Hay, or feel a yearning to possess something called Général Kleber (except Mrs Kleber), Adam Messerich, Zigeuner Knaber, *Rosa scabrosa*, Hamburg, Grüss an Aachen, *Rosa longiscuspis*, F. J. Grootendorst or Zéphirine Drouhin, all of which are lovely roses? But really, if you come to think of it, are these any worse (though admittedly they are mostly longer) than the names of many modern varieties like Fanny Blankers Koen, Mainzer Wappen, Spartan, Sunday Press, Konrad Adenauer, Fred Loads and Percy Thrower (with respect to the names' real owners), Fervid, Interview, Mullard Jubilee or Scrabo. There was even an HT not too many years ago called Billy Boiler.

But names or no, the old roses are coming back fast. One school of thought gives as the reason that people are becoming tired of what they describe as the strident colours of modern roses. Most of the old roses are certainly fairly muted, but many of the newer shrubs for which there is an increasing demand are just as bright, so that cannot be the only reason. I, and it would seem, many other people, like both kinds, each in its way. I like Super Star (apart from its recently acquired propensity to mildew), which at once puts me among the vulgarians, but I also like *Rosa rubrifolia* or, say, Felicité Parmentier with its wonderful rosettes of palest creamy blush. A good, screaming red can look right in the right place.

Some people admire the airy delicacy found in many of the old roses, particularly some of the species, and say that a modern rose bush is not a thing of beauty when out of flower. This is true in the main, but against it many modern roses have much better foliage than many of the old ones.

All these are probably partial reasons, but I think myself that a strong factor has been the increasing interest in what we like to think of as the more gracious ways of living in the past, and particularly at the moment in the Victorian age. This has made people delve backwards in horticulture as well as in other things, and suddenly rose lovers have woken up to what they have been missing. Everyone is also thinking in terms of labour-saving gardens, which has increased the interest in shrubs in general, and many are looking for something other than the inevitable lilac, forsythia and mock orange. Shrub roses can fill most needs and fill your garden with beauty, whatever size it may be.

We must all be grateful for the patient and devoted work of people like Mr Graham Thomas, Gardens Adviser to the National Trust, Miss Murrell now retired from her nursery in Shrewsbury, and a few others who have always known the truth and who have helped to keep the old roses going and make available to us many that would otherwise have been lost for ever.

CHAPTER 2

A Brief Look into Rose History

IT is surprising that so many Victorian clergymen were devoted to the rose, for its history resembles one vast, botanical orgy. No one can be sure who is whose father or mother, and this makes the accurate production of a family tree almost impossible.

I have seen estimates of the number of true rose species, which vary between about two hundred and less than one hundred and fifty, but at any rate there are not all that many. The confusion in this case comes from the fact that a number of the so-called species (an original, wild rose that will come true from seed) are certainly subspecies, resulting from crosses between rose species growing in the wild. Both kinds get lumbered with Latin names, and are the oldest roses of all.

Later crossing, both natural and that done by rose growers of which they kept no record, has made the situation even more chaotic, though as I mentioned in the last chapter, a number of dedicated enthusiasts have performed many miracles in sorting out the tangle. There are, however, large areas of uncertainty left, which leads to a good deal of confusion about classification in catalogues and elsewhere. Trying to place some of the roses is like driving round a strange city, looking for somewhere to put your car, with Mr Thomas, in his Warden's hat, pencil poised, telling you you can't park here.

If two members of two different groups of roses are crossed, where do you put the result, particularly if it does not much resemble either group? Take, for instance, the rose called Conrad Ferdinand Meyer. This is an enormous, rather gaunt grower with very double light pink blooms, more like a hybrid perpetual than anything else, and which is in fact a cross between a climbing Tea Rose called Gloire de Dijon and one of the Rugosa family. How can it possibly belong to the same group as Pink Grootendorst, which has reasonably compact, bushy growth and clusters of tiny, bright pink flowers with their petals fringed like a pink or Sweet William? The botanists' answer in this case would seem to be in the foliage, for both have the deeply creased leaves of the Rugosa family and both are classed as Rugosa roses. Generally, where there is a definitely known cross, or at the very least a suspected one, a rose is grouped with the parent whose characteristics are dominant.

In other cases, though, I am sure that roses have been put into a group simply because, it would seem, they have to go somewhere. This is surely borne out by the fact that more is occasionally found out about one or other of them and it is rescued and returned to its own family. Mr Thomas's work in tracking down the true Musk Rose is a case in point, and verified the argument long put forward by some that Shakespeare's Musk Rose was not the true Musk Rose at all (the latter came from the East a good deal later) but one of our native wild roses.

All of which is leading up to something.

In the short introduction for each group of roses that I describe in Chapter 5 and onwards, I have tried to give the general characteristics of the group, size, type of flowers, habit of growth, soil preferences and so on. Perhaps the first and second rose, as you read through the details of the varieties that follow each introduction, will make sense of this, but then suddenly at number three or four, what have we here? Turn back the page. I thought so; this is nonsense. It may seem so, but do not blame me. You can at this point wave your hands vaguely, like P. G. Wodehouse's Hon. Galahad Threepwood after a tour of the rose garden, and say "Roses and – er – roses, and all that sort of thing", and leave it at that. But what a lot you will miss. Gradually, if you persevere, the exceptions will stand out as exceptions, and things will make sense.

Now into history proper, condensed for your sake and mine.

As I have said, the oldest roses of all are the true species, which go back into unrecorded history. No one knows just how far, but fossil remains in Europe and America have established their existence millions of years ago. They have always grown only to the north of the equator, and all the true species have single flowers. It is rather interesting that the rose is one of the few

flowers to be considered to be more beautiful by the majority of
people (though not by me) in its double form, and that roses seem
particularly prone to produce double blooms when different
species are crossed. Thus a large number of the earliest garden
roses, a lot of which are naturally occurring hybrids, are double.
This was pure quirk of nature and not design, for intentional
crossing did not start until comparatively recent times. Another
odd fact in passing is that double roses seem to have larger petals
than most single ones. I do not know the reason for that.

Probably only about fifteen species or sub-species have con-
tributed to the development of the garden rose. Of these fifteen,
Rosa gallica or the Gallica Rose is thought to be the one from
which all our European garden roses are descended, with other
roses now and again chipping in. No one knows the date of the
first Gallicas, but at some time R. *gallica* was crossed with another
species, possibly one of the Musk Rose family, to produce R.
damascena, the Damask Rose. This eventually came to Europe
from Asia, perhaps brought to England by the Crusaders from
the neighbourhood of Damascus. It was and still is the rose
mainly used for the production of attar of roses in Bulgaria,
Turkey, Persia and India, and is also the rose depicted on the
walls of the Palace of Knossos in Crete, dating from about
2000 BC.

Crossing of the Damask Rose with R. *canina*, our own Dog
Rose, very early on, is generally considered to have produced the
Alba Roses, though Svend Poulsen, the Danish hybridist, has
raised some doubts about this by finding some Albas coming true
from seed. Yet another series of crosses over a period of more
than a hundred years, and involving probably at least four species,
produced the Centifolias, which do not seem to have played as
big a part in the subsequent development of garden roses as most
of the others. They were brought to perfection in Holland about
the beginning of the eighteenth century, became famous as the
roses painted in many masterpieces by the old Dutch painters, and
in due course they sported the Moss Roses. This means that at
some stage a Centifolia rose grew a branch on which the flower
stalks and buds had a strange, moss-like growth, which was
considered attractive enough to propagate from, and a new family

of roses came into existence, not through cross pollination, but by a freak of nature. Other roses throughout history have sported branches with flowers different from the parent and many wonderful varieties have been created in this way. In many cases it is the mixed ancestry of the parent rose that is coming out in a different form, though there is no record of any rose earlier than the Centifolia sport having the moss-like growth on it.

All these families of roses, including the species and with the single exception of one Damask, the Autumn Damask, were once-flowering only, and even the Autumn Damask's late summer display was (and is) pretty fitful.

It was not until the eighteenth century that R. *chinensis*, in the form of a red rose which is really perpetual flowering from June to September, was introduced into the west, not surprisingly in view of its name, from China, where perpetual flowering roses had long been established. The crossing of a variety of this China rose, Parson's Pink China, with the Autumn Damask gave us the first of the Bourbon race of roses in 1823. This cross took place by accident when the two roses were growing side by side in a hedge on the Isle du Bourbon (now Réunion) in the Indian Ocean. Spotted by a French botanist, the merits of the new variety were quickly recognised, particularly the fact that it was recurrent. It was taken to France and extensively developed there until, in 1837, the Bourbon was again crossed with another offspring of a Chinese and Autumn Damask cross, a small family called the Portland Roses, which originated in Italy but were called after the Duchess of Portland of that time. This Portland rose, combined with the Bourbon, resulted in the first Hybrid Perpetual, which was the first major group of roses really to bear some resemblance to our modern HTs and was more-or-less repeat-flowering, though it was certainly not perpetual.

A little later the rather delicate Tea Rose arrived, like the China Rose from the east. This, conjoined with the Hybrid Perpetuals, gave us the Hybrid Teas, the further development of which really takes us beyond the historical scope of this book except that a few modern HTs can be used as shrubs. But there is one further development that I touched on briefly in the first chapter that should be here expanded on a little.

Until the late 1860s, little more than a hundred years ago, all our garden roses had been pink, white, or crimson. A few of the roses of Chinese origin had blooms of a pale cream, but apart from one or two species, mostly single, there were no bright yellows or flame colours. It was at this time that Pernet-Ducher in his nursery in Lyons began a long series of experimental crossings with the wild Persian yellow rose (R. *foetida*). At last, in 1900, by crossing it with a Hybrid Perpetual called Antoine Ducher, he achieved the break he was looking for in Soleil d'Or, which had flowers like a Hybrid Perpetual and was of a rich orange-yellow, shaded nasturtium red. From this one rose are descended all our bright yellow and orange garden roses, right up to such modern shrubs as Fred Loads and Chinatown.

So far I have not mentioned the Rugosa roses, originating in a species from Japan and China, but they do not figure very much in the historical line of garden roses. They went along very much on their own, from time to time producing some interesting hybrids, but generally speaking not being particularly sociable.

So much for straight, chronological history. There are many branches of the tree I have not followed as I have concentrated only on the main lines of development. If you want to delve deeper, read some of the books which are described in Chapter 18 or which are listed in the bibliography. The purpose of this book is, in the main, to tell people how to grow shrub roses and I want no one to be in the position of James Thurber's small girl, who was given a book on penguins to read by her teacher. Presently she came back and said: "This book tells me more about penguins than I want to know." So we will conclude with a chart, which may help. It is on the next page.

The rest of this chapter is still historical, but is made up of more or less connected jottings. For instance, the Greeks and the Romans were great ones for roses and both Theophrastus and Pliny wrote quite extensively about them. The former, the so-called Father of Botany, made what must be the first mention of pruning when he wrote: "If a bush be burned or cut over it bears better flowers." This mention of burning over has caused much speculation as to its meaning. Burning rose bushes would certainly not be recommended nowadays, though it is possible a suckering

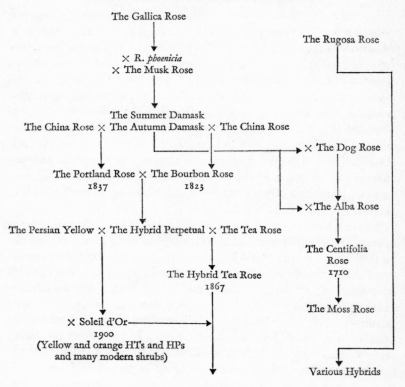

family like the Scotch Roses or the Gallicas might survive beneath the ground and send up new shoots in the spring. A writer in the American Rose Annual suggests that a true translation of what Theophrastus said indicated trimming of the bushes and then singeing the ends of the canes to prevent bleeding and the entry of disease, which may be the answer. Theophrastus also mentions taking cuttings.

Roses were, of course, common in his time all round the Mediterranean. The name Rose comes from the Celtic word *rhodd*, meaning red, and the Island of Rhodes took its name because of the huge numbers of roses which grew wild there. Both Romans and Greeks used vast quantities at their feasts and festivals, spending huge sums of money on them and even having blooms brought from North Africa, though no one now knows how they were kept fresh on the journey. This pagan association with the rose barred it from use in the Christian church over a long period but then, in common with a number of once pagan rites, the rose in some way became so respectable that it was adopted as the emblem of the martyrs. Maybe its beauty could not be resisted.

Pliny is on record as saying that: "Those who try to get their roses early, dig a trench about a foot deep about the roots, pouring in warm water as the cup is beginning to bud" – a point to be noted by present-day exhibitors, but Pliny said it, not me. He also, in his *Natural History*, apparently described the Centifolia as we know it today, though the modern authority, Dr C. C. Hurst, has now proved that it did not arrive on the scene until the eighteenth century. "The number of petals, which is never less than five." Pliny said, when talking about roses generally, "goes on increasing in amount, till one finds one variety with as many as a hundred and these are known as *centifolias*." Either Pliny was describing a completely different rose or he could not count.

But at least it would seem that he really did mean petals, for care is needed with some of the ancient writers as they referred to leaves as petals. And yet another source of confusion can be that writers right up to about 1800 made no distinction between pinks and reds, which does not help the identification of old varieties from written contemporary descriptions.

One final note on the Romans before we leave them. They believed the root of R. *canina* to be of benefit in the treatment of hydrophobia and hence, in all probability, came the name Dog Rose.

Roses were popular in England in the Middle Ages for decorating churches and shrines, and also in heraldry. The Alba or white rose is the Rose of York and R. *gallica officinalis* is the Lancastrian Rose. The Tudor Rose was derived as the result of the amalgamation of York and Lancaster after the Wars of the Roses as everyone knows, but what we know as the York and Lancaster Rose, a mixture of pink and white petals, was not, it appears, known in this country until the late 1600s, a good long time after Shakespeare's celebrated ceremony was supposed to have taken place. A pity, if true.

It was not for a very long time that it was realised that plants had sexes, so that no breeding of new varieties of roses was carried out except by chance crossings in the wild. During the seventeenth, eighteenth and nineteenth centuries, however, artificial breeding of roses was gradually developed, mainly in France and the Low Countries. Not much was done in Great Britain until the nineteenth century, but this did not stop people giving expert opinions on various aspects of the subject. Gerard, in his *Greate Herballe* of 1597, wrote:

"The yellow rose which (as divers do report) was by Art so coloured and altered from its first estate by grafting a wilde Rose upon a broome stalke, where by (they say) it doth not only change its colour but its smell. By my own part, having found contrary by my own experience I cannot be induced to believe the report." I once tried it to see what would happen. Believe it or not, he's right.

The author of *The Gentleman's Recreation, Graffeing, and the Art of Gardening*, written in 1654, was after the evergreen rose. "For to graffe the Rose," he said, "that he should keepe all the year greene, some do take and cleave the holly and do graffe in a red or white Rosebud and then put clay or mosse to him and let him grow. And some put the Rosebud into a slit in the bark and so put clay or mosse and bind him featly therein and let him grow and he shall carry the leaf all the year."

What the writer does not seem to have thought of is that he might have revolutionised Christmas by producing holly with large red or white flowers, two-inch berries, and black spot.

And finally, just to show that there is nothing new under the sun, in the late 1800s, Richard Jefferies was writing in *Amaryllis at the Fair*: "Not only are there no damask roses, but there is no place for them nowadays." That might have been written by any shrub rose enthusiast during the last twenty years. Fortunately it is no longer true.

CHAPTER 3

Getting the Best Out of Them

DEAN HOLE, one of the Victorian clergymen I mentioned in the second chapter and one of the founders of the National Rose Society (now Royal), said in his *A Book About Roses*, "There should be beds of Roses, banks of Roses, bowers of Roses, hedges of Roses, edgings of Roses, pillars of Roses, arches of Roses, fountains of Roses, baskets of Roses, vistas and alleys of Roses. Now overhead, now at our feet, they should creep and climb." He could have added (at the sacrifice of poetry) that you could be eating a jam sandwich of rose hep jam while you are looking at it, but he is right. So there should be – if you can afford it, and if your garden is at least a quarter of an acre in size. Nowadays we have to be more practical.

However, whatever ideal you are aiming at, it will not be achieved by sticking the roses in any old how and any old where. A good deal of thought should be given to planning, though I am not going to draw a lot of theoretical plans that will not fit anybody's garden except by luck. Maybe an idea or two for single beds to show what goes well with what would be helpful, and they could be easily adapted to the actual shapes and sizes to fit your garden. Anything more detailed or an overall planting scheme really has to be drawn up on the spot. Such natural features as background trees and the position and shape of a house can change the whole conception, and in any case it is much more fun to make one's own mistakes than to let someone else make them for you – in gardening, anyway. Rectifying them and making gradual changes is the only real way to learn.

What follows in the rest of this chapter will, I hope, be helpful when you come to draw your own plans, even if they are only in your head as most people's plans are, but there are one or two general points to make first.

All roses need plenty of water but good drainage. They need

sunlight and air, but do not like draughts or howling gales. Do not, therefore, put them where you would a water-lily or a windmill.

Maybe the best way to deal with ideas for planting is to go through the various groups of roses described in Chapters 5-16, at least where there is something special to say about a variety, and to indicate some of the ways they can be used to make the most of them. There will be many roses I do not mention specifically, but this does not mean that the ones I do name are necessarily better; just that the book would be twice its present length if I did. You can, of course, substitute one Moss Rose or one Gallica for another if you wish, but check its habit of growth and size first.

Starting with the species or near species, it should be said straight away that the majority of these are too big for a very small garden and are probably only suitable as single specimens in a medium-sized one. Almost without exception they flower only once – and this can be fleeting – though some have gay autumn heps which are an added attraction. If you only have limited room you will want to make sure you are getting value for money and it is probably better to choose a rose that flowers more than once. The only roses that do this in my list of species are Stanwell Perpetual, which is worth anybody's money and can be kept to a reasonable size, Frühlingsmorgen, and Nevada and its pink sport Marguerite Hilling, all of which are really large.

Many of the species flower very early, even starting in a favourable year at the end of April, and five of these are in my list, Canarybird, R. *ecea*, Ormiston Roy, R. *headleyensis* and R. Highdownensis. The first three can be kept to a moderate size by judicious pruning and more particularly so if grown as standards, in which form Canarybird is very often sold. R. *ecea* is the smallest, upright, and does not spread out much. All are at their best if planted in front of a dark evergreen and where they can be viewed from the house. Such a background heightens their beauty by contrast and you can see them even if you do not feel like strolling out of doors so early in the year.

The Persian Roses, R. *foetida persiana* and R. *foetida bicolor* are not particularly robust growers, need good soil and cultivation, and are probably at their best with some wall shelter. Not, I think, for anyone with limited space as their flowers, though some of the most spectacular of all roses, are short-lived. A heavy shower can shatter them and that is that for the year. They have no great beauty afterwards.

For some reason the Penzance Briers appear regularly, often as a class on their own, in the catalogues of nurseries which only have a very limited selection of shrub roses. They have their charm if you live in a mansion, but even there you would not, I think, if you made them your first choice of shrub roses, become an addict wanting more. They are all hybrids of R. *rubiginosa*, which is our native Sweet Brier, and were produced by Lord Penzance in the late 1800s as a hobby. There were some sixteen varieties originally and he named most of them after heroines of Sir Walter Scott's novels. Many of them were very similar and only a limited selection of the best is now available.

They make large, thorny shrubs which can spread by suckering and which need careful placing even in a big garden, as they are of no great beauty after the mainly single flowers are over at the end of June. The foliage does not age attractively, but the striking point about it is that, like the flowers, it is scented. Strolling past a Penzance Brier on a warm evening after a shower, and perhaps crushing one of the leaves, can be quite a sensual experience.

These roses are often recommended for hedges when, planted three feet apart, they can be kept by pruning and training to five feet or so instead of their more normal six to eight feet. The hedges will certainly keep things in or out, but though they do have smallish red or orange heps in the autumn as well as their flowers earlier, their period of real beauty is brief. A hedge made from the wild roses you see growing in the countryside would give much the same effect, though the Penzance roses have a wider colour range and have rather larger blossoms.

I can think of better hedging plants – better hedging roses for that matter – and to me the best way that they can be grown is to have one or two in a not too prominent (though sunny) place in a group of other shrubs where their companions can take over when they leave off. Allow them plenty of room to spread and keep a lookout for black spot.

The smaller varieties of the Scotch or Burnet roses, R. *spinosissima* Double Yellow, for instance (which is not in my list, but I had to stop somewhere), sucker freely and associate very well with heathers and cistus on wild banks where they are free to ramble. They will grow in the poorest of soils and can even be used most attractively for capping a dry-stone wall. Their suckers will spread between the stones and the shoots emerge from all sorts of unexpected places, the yellow flowers hanging down in golden festoons. Their flowering season is not a long one, but the foliage is small with a fern-like attraction and even in winter the canes have a warm bronze tone to them which is pleasing.

Do not try the wall treatment with the larger *spinosissima* hybrids however. Frühlingsgold, for instance, would have the wall down in a season. It makes instead a magnificent specimen planting, sometimes as much as eight or nine feet tall and six to seven feet across, covered in June with huge, nearly single creamy flowers. It is a fast grower, too, attaining its full size in two or three years.

One species, R. *paulii rosea*, is a low, spreading ground coverer

PLATE 3

Species and their hybrids   *page*

1. *multibracteata*   70
2. *paulii rosea*   71
3. *pomifera duplex*   71
4. *rubiginosa* 'Amy Robsart' 71
5. *rubiginosa* 'Lady Penzance' 72
6. *rubiginosa* 'Lord Penzance' 72
7. *rubiginosa* 'Meg Merrilees' 72
8. *rubrifolia*   72
9. *sericea pteracantha*   72

for the front of the shrubbery, or else it should be used to hang down a steep bank or over a wall built, perhaps, where a lawn changes levels.

The Alba Roses are mostly large, upright shrubs and make up one of the groups which have especially attractive leaves of a slate blue or grey-green colour. They are invaluable for group planting or for use as single specimens, one or two only being of a size suitable for a small garden. They will mix well with most of the other old roses and the leafy mounds they form when out of flower can make a good background for other perpetual flowering kinds. The largest Albas will happily scramble over walls or up through the branches of even taller neighbours like a large holly or one of the bigger varieties of *philadelphus*.

The Gallicas on the other hand are mainly short growing and are especially noted for their gay and often striped flowers, held erect above the generally upright and thornless stems. At or near the front of a shrub border, in a garden of any size, is one good place for them. They can spread by sucker growth, particularly if they are on their own roots, so this should be allowed for, though

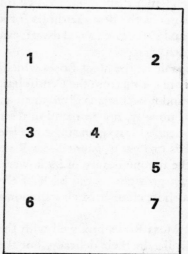

PLATE 4

Species and their hybrids   page

I have never found them as rampant in this respect as the Scotch Roses. As low hedging plants they are most striking and they can be quite easily kept neat by pruning and clipping over, to which they take more kindly than some. They are tough and reliable.

A number of people hold the view that Centifolia roses are not good garden plants, and they certainly can be rather ungainly and untidy. Many make large, lax shrubs, rather open and with big, drooping leaves, but the huge, globular, many-petalled and richly scented blooms, which also droop, are something no flower-lover should miss. You can solve the problem to some extent by concentrating on the smaller, more compact varieties, but it is as well, even then, to plant them with other roses – perhaps some of the Albas – on which they can lean for support. I have found that four or five stout three-foot stakes stuck into the ground round each plant, fairly close in to the centre, and with green, plastic-covered garden wire strung tautly between them, make good leaning material which is quickly hidden once the leaves come out.

The more vigorous Centifolias like Robert le Diable and Tour de Malakoff will make good pillar roses, obtaining the support they need that way, and you can then look up into the centre of the nodding blooms, which is much better than looking down on them from the top. Petite de Hollande is the best Centifolia for a small garden for general planting, and De Meaux, a real dwarf, can be fitted happily into the rock garden.

Much of the above could also be said of the Moss Roses which, as you may or may not remember, are sports from the Centifolias. But here the mossing of the buds and flower stems gives them an added attraction and the appeal of novelty, not to mention their sentimental associations. Careful selection can again single out the more compact growers, but there is one great, gaunt Moss Rose which should not be missed for the unique beauty of its flowers. This is William Lobb, which must go right to the back of the border, or better still be used as a short climber or all its blooms will end up in the mud.

Neither the Centifolias nor the Moss Roses mix well with the species, whose charm in the main lies in their delicacy, but the same would not, I think, be said of the China Roses. They are mainly rather short, spindly shrubs, small enough in the case of

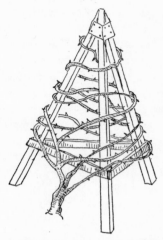

Pyramid for bourbons and others

Little White Pet and Natalie Nypels for a place on the rockery, but not too close to De Meaux, which might look clumsy by comparison. I have used both kinds on the same rockery, but grouped them well apart so that there is no conflict.

Some China Roses can be used effectively for bedding in a small bed. I say small because, although they are continuous flowering, they will make a dainty rather than spectacular show, something to be appreciated from fairly close to rather than as a bold splash of colour. Their small, pointed foliage is attractive as well.

Bloomfield Abundance is the giant of the China clan and will top eight feet, smothered in its tiny, immaculately-shaped, pale pink blooms. It really needs another shrub to scramble through and this is where a Penzance Brier might come in useful.

For a really unusual bed, one that will cause no end of comment, plant a bush of R. *rubrifolia* (from the species list) in the centre and surround it with five or six of the China hybrid or mutation R. *viridiflora*, the Green Rose. The plum-purple leaves and stems of R. *rubrifolia* and later its pinky-red clusters of heps, with the continuously produced green, purple and brown flowers of R.

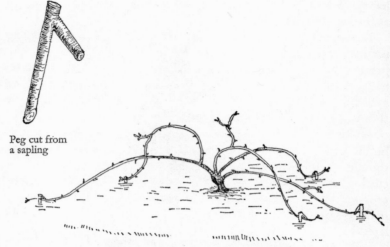

Peg cut from
a sapling

Pegging down a hybrid perpetual

viridiflora will cause an acute case of *flower arangea viridaeyea* among
your friends.

The Bourbon Roses make lusty open shrubs or short pillar
roses and many have the full, quartered blooms so much admired
in the old roses. They can be ungainly, not so much from general
laxness of growth as with the Centifolias, as from strong but
rather undisciplined canes which may need support of a different
kind. A three-sided pyramid of wooden laths or thin larch poles,
with side bracing pieces half-way up, and with the long, fairly
stiff shoots of the rose trained round and up this makes a change
from a pillar and is a good way of enforcing discipline. The
pyramid can, of course, be used for other roses, too.

Hybrid Perpetuals are basically not unlike HTs but they are
mostly too vigorous for bedding in the ordinary sense. So try
pegging them down, something that is not often seen nowadays
except in the gardens of some of the old stately homes.

Each year varieties like Frau Karl Druschki, Hugh Dickson,
George Dickson, Ulrich Brunner and Général Jacqueminot
(these are all Hybrid Perpetuals, though you may find one
or two of them listed in some catalogues as HTs) will send

up very strong four, five or even six foot shoots. If these are left to grow naturally they will look ungainly and flower mainly at the top. So peg them down.

This means arching over each shoot of not less than half an inch in diameter at its base, so that its tip almost touches the ground, and tying it there to a wooden peg or, where appropriate, to the base of a neighbouring plant. The bending must be done gently so that there is no chance of snapping off or kinking the shoots and one should try to spread them out as evenly as possible over the bed. When they are pegged like this, practically every bud along the length of each shoot will produce at least one bloom, though they will not generally have stalks long enough for cutting. A bed covered with these gently bowed shoots, criss-crossing each other in an intricate pattern, can produce a really magnificent display in July with a rather less magnificent one later.

In March of each year, cut back some of the old shoots and, instead of pruning them as well, simply peg down the vigorous new ones that have grown to take their place, removing only two or three inches at the tips which will probably be unripe. If a good new shoot has appeared from half-way along an old one, treat it as you would a rambler, and cut back the old one only to where the new one has sprouted.

The second flowering of Hybrid Perpetuals is not always very prolific, and in any case there is always a longish gap with no flowers after the first flush. The cure for both these problems is to grow clematis of the *viticella* group through them. These can be cut back about a foot from the ground each year at the same time as the roses are pruned and so be prevented from becoming an all-embracing tangle. The pink clematis Comtesse de Bouchard flowers from mid-June to August and others which would suit are Perle d'Azur (light blue), W. E. Gladstone (mid-blue), and Margo Koster (deep pink). It is probably best to let the roses grow for a year or two first to build up some sort of framework for the clematis, which can, of course, be used effectively with other tall-growing shrub roses to give colour late in the season if the roses are once-flowering only. If the colours are chosen so that they blend, there is no reason why you could not have them

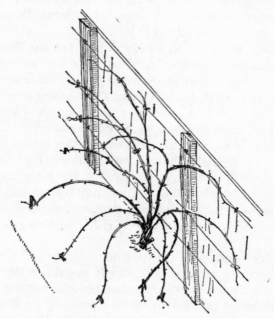

Combined pegging down and training on fence

flowering at the same time as well, which means that you can introduce a wide range of blues into your overall scheme.

One warning. If you intend to do no more than the minimum of pruning of your roses (I am talking now about shrub roses in general) it would be as well to choose clematis of the *patens* type, like Nellie Moser or Marie Boisselot. These are not so vigorous and only need the old flowers and dead shoots removed, and they will not become a tangle which could overwhelm the roses in a few years. Whichever type of clematis you choose, black spot spray for the rose is said to help against clematis wilt, and mildew and insect spray against mildew and aphis on both types of plant.

But back to Hybrid Perpetuals. Should you decide to grow them against a fence, the shoots on the side nearest to it can be trained to grow along and up it, and the ones in front can be pegged down to the ground. This needs quite a wide bed.

Or again, with the less vigorous varieties like Mrs John Laing,

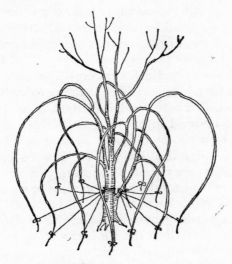

Tying or pegging down to own base

you can bend down some of the longest outer shoots and tie them into the base of the plant itself. This can also be done with any of them if they are grown on their own and will greatly increase the display of flowers and stop the rose getting bare at the base, though it may look rather odd for a few weeks before the leaves come.

Hybrid Perpetuals are very hardy, but do repay good cultivation, and you should be prepared to spray against mildew. If really pushed to it, they can stand some shade, but they must have sun for some part of the day.

Even if your skills are such as to qualify you for the post of Head Gardener to the House of Usher, you could hardly fail to succeed with the good-tempered Rugosas. They will thrive almost anywhere and on the poorest soils, and they are certainly the finest of all roses for foliage. Blanc Double de Coubert and Roseraie de l'Hay, to name only two, are the first roses in spring to show green when their luxuriant, crinkled, bright, fresh green leaves begin to unfurl. In the autumn these turn to a striking yellow and stay like this for some weeks before they fall.

As specimen shrubs all Rugosas are grand and are seldom out of flower right through the summer. It is only a pity that so many of them have been saddled with either difficult or ugly names.

As well as the two mentioned above we have Conrad Ferdinand Meyer, Frau Dagmar Hastrup (or Hartop), F. J. Grootendorst, Max Graf, Scabrosa and Schneezwerg – Dracula's Daughters to a man, and what a handicap when it comes to sales.

Rugosas, together with the Hybrid Musk Roses, probably make the best medium-sized to tall hedges. By this I mean that they will make something more closely resembling what most of us think of as a hedge than other roses. Rose hedges tend to be exuberant, rather sprawling barriers many feet wide, very beautiful, but only suitable for the largest gardens or parks, though one could make an exception in the case of the parade ground erectness of the floribunda Queen Elizabeth. If left to their own devices, many Rugosas will follow the same, spreading pattern, but they can be more easily controlled than some, though even so you must allow for four feet or so of width. They will stand, and in fact benefit from, light clipping over with shears in winter, though the treatment must be nothing like as severe as that which you would give to a beech or privet hedge.

Suckering, and Rugosas are prone to this, can be a problem and the width of the hedge could gradually increase because of it. However, if the plants are not on their own roots, and such suckers as do appear are removed promptly at their source, they need not be too serious a menace. Do not simply cut them off at ground level or they will come up again like daisies.

Your Rugosa hedge will be well clothed with leaves right down to the ground if you choose varieties like *alba*, Roseraie de l'Hay, Agnes, Frau Dagmar Hastrup, Schneezwerg and Scabrosa. The two Grootendorsts and Blanc Double de Coubert will be a little more open at the base, but cutting back of some of the main growths to seven or eight inches every other year or so will encourage branching lower down. All of them will make good seaside screens as salty breezes do them no harm.

There are three other Rugosa hybrids which can also be used for hedges, but they need different treatment and are more difficult to keep neat and tidy if that is what you want. These are Conrad Ferdinand Meyer and its sport, Nova Zembla (a little less vigorous than its parent), and Sarah Van Fleet. They will shoot up to eight or ten feet, really need some support, and also need their rather gaunt and bare lower halves hidden, like the children's toys behind the sofa. In other words they are roses for background hedges, at the rear of a border perhaps, with something else growing to a height of three or four feet in front of them. Above that level they will give a breathtaking display of bloom with two main flushes, in June and July, and again in the autumn. Unfortunately these three have not inherited the Rugosa virtual immunity to pests and diseases. Conrad Ferdinand Meyer particularly should not be grown in a district where rose rust is prevalent.

All Rugosas are incredibly prickly and need a pruning approach like that of a gladiator entering the ring. I once did a prickle count on one inch of a fairly thick stem of Pink Grootendorst and the total came to seventy-five. Multiplying this out after counting the number of main branches and measuring their length, and taking an approximation for the smaller branches and twigs, the total came to 140,000 for the whole bush – and it was not fully grown. As a hedge, it would stop anything that had not got the hide of a rhinoceros.

Finally to the odd man out amongst the Rugosas. This is Max Graf, a Rugosa crossed with a rambler, one of the so-called ground-cover roses. I have reservations about their use in this way, unless the ground around the bushes is kept completely clear of weeds until the roses have really started to spread. And weeds can get a hold even after that during the winter months when the leaves of the roses have fallen, though fairly heavy mulching with grass cuttings, which can be shaken down reasonably easily through the interlacing branches, will help to keep them in check. Weeding a fully developed Max Graf can be like putting your hand into a tank of piranha fish, and it is better to my mind to drape it down a bank where weeding is not needed, or down over a low wall, where it can ramble at will, rooting as it goes. It is not a substitute for St John's Wort or periwinkle.

The Hybrid Musk Roses are another versatile group, that will make marvellous informal hedges about five feet high and four wide if given selective pruning. By this I mean the removal or shortening of the occasional rogue growth in winter, for most of the Hybrid Musks have a habit of sending out the odd enormous shoot, laden with flowers in late summer, but at totally unexpected angles.

You can if you wish plant a mixture of varieties in your hedge, but Prosperity and Vanity are more vigorous than the others and should not be included with the rest. In the other direction, Danae and Thisbe and Felicia are lower and more spreading. Magenta, which has, because of rather different ancestry, flowers more resembling a Bourbon, flops all over the place and is not a hedging rose at all. It should be planted among other roses that can give it support.

Hybrid Musk Roses can be used for bedding and treated like very vigorous and tall-growing floribundas – that is, they should be given only fairly light pruning. They do, however, spread out wide, and three feet at least is needed between each plant. Do not expect such a wide range of colours as with the modern floribundas, for apart from a few comparatively recent crimson and scarlet varieties, most are in the pastel shades. But within their range, you will get even greater profusion of bloom and a wonderful scent which no floribunda can match.

The modern shrub roses are such a mixed bag that it is impossible to generalise about their use. When I describe each in detail later, I also give some indication of any special qualities, or uses where these exist.

I can, however, say something now about the climbers and ramblers, and undoubtedly the best way of growing most of the older varieties is to let them wander up trees, or through really tough, large, evergreen shrubs. The dark foliage of holly, cypress and yew, and the greyish-green of some junipers, sets off a climbing rose as does nothing else, and covers the bare stems of the rose in winter. But if you have no evergreens suitable, do not worry. Old apple or pear trees make a very good second best. However, make sure that they are not rotten, and likely to collapse, for the weight of one of these roses when fully grown can be tremendous, as can the force of a gale of wind blowing against it.

Some of the more vigorous shrubs will also climb quite happily in the same way and ramble through the branches like an MP who has been asked an awkward question, though not as far as the real climbers. The support of a tree – or perhaps in some cases simply the urge to reach the light – seems to give many roses added vigour, and the sight of the huge, massed, hundred-bloom sprays of such rampant growers as R. *filipes* 'Kiftsgate' or R. *longiscuspis* hanging in scented curtains from the branches of a tall holly is an experience no one can ever forget.

Climbers and ramblers can, of course, also be used for arches (some I list are rather big for this), pergolas, or to grow on one side of a wall, when they will tumble over the top (better still if your neighbour's rose tumbles over the top of your wall), and for covering unsightly sheds and summerhouses, which they will help to keep cool in summer. The shorter kinds can be grown on pillars, to give height perhaps in the middle of a bed of other roses, or on their own as specimens, but always taking care to train the canes round the pillars in a spiral to encourage side shoots to break low down. Otherwise most of the flowers will cluster at the top.

And now for some of the other shrubs and plants that associate well with roses and can be used with them in a mixed planting, particularly where the roses themselves flower only once. Grey or grey-green leaved plants always look well with the old roses. Rosemary is first-rate and when fully grown can give the much needed support to the more lax Mosses, Centifolias and others – and of course it has its own quiet blue flowers, in addition to being a herb you can use in the kitchen. The common and the purple-leaved sages are other good herbs for the foreground or for infilling, as is lavender. Other plants and small shrubs include pinks, cotton lavender (*Santolina chamaecyparissus* – believe it or not), the blue *Ceanothus, Solanum crispum*, shrubby potentillas (not all grey-leaved, but continuously in flower from July onwards and not unlike the yellow species roses themselves), *Alchemilla*, hostas, *Anaphalis yedoensis* and *Stachys lantana. Cytisus battandieri*, the pineapple broom, is another grey-leaved shrub that I have used successfully with old roses, but do not expect it to support them unless you have managed to grow a specimen like the one on Battle Hill at the Royal Horticultural Society gardens at

Wisley in Surrey. This must be twelve or fifteen feet across, growing in the open, but generally it tends to be a bit lanky and tender, liking the protection of a wall, though mine is in a fairly open spot and used as an effective backing for R. *moyesii* 'Geranium'. *Euonymus radicans* is another good shrub.

Japanese anemones, columbines and foxgloves all look well planted among shrub roses and all tolerate some shade. So do some of the common lilies like Regale and the various forms of L. *speciosum*. The erect habit of growth of all these, and also their flower forms make for a pleasing contrast, and I much prefer them to under-planting with real ground-coverers like pansies and violas, which are often recommended but which can make mulching and proper cultivation of the roses difficult. In any case, the latter get smothered in time if used with many shrub roses where the canes arch outwards, while the taller lilies and anemones will push up through them.

Clematis we have already dealt with.

One of the most attractive settings for shrub roses is in a large heather bed. Choose the more upright and airy growers like the Moyesii family and a number of the other species, Golden Wings, Madame Hardy, Pink Grootendorst or Blanc Double de Coubert (which, though hardly airy, is not too dense at the base), as the heather likes the sun just as much as the roses and must not be too much in the shade. Allow a circle of at least three feet round each rose for mulching. The taller growing heathers will give some support to some of the smaller lax-growing roses.

Shrub roses, as I have said several times already, make beautiful specimens growing on their own, but there are one or two points worth making about this use for them. If you pick a spot in the middle of a lawn, do not forget that you will have to cut the grass round it. So choose your rose carefully. Avoid those that sucker freely or they will take over the lawn. If you choose one with long, arching canes, cut a square in the turf (easier to cut round than a circle) that will keep you and the mower reasonably clear of it – or be prepared to lose an eye or two. Something like Canarybird, R. *multibracteata*, R. *forrestiana* or Frühlingsgold on a windy day will grab at you like a tax inspector with ferret's teeth.

I prefer to find a corner, perhaps at the junction of two hedges, for my roses of this sort, and provided that they are planted at least three feet away from the hedge they will do famously. The drawback is that you cannot admire your rose from all directions, but at least you have the eyes to admire it with. There are plenty of roses that you can quite safely plant on their own on a lawn, Chinatown, the Hybrid Musks, Bonn, Berlin, Fred Loads and many of the older ones. It is a question of noting their habit of growth and their ultimate size and picking your rose accordingly.

For group planting of roses along the side of a lawn it is often more effective to mix your varieties, taking into account height, spread and colour. The more strident modern floribunda-type shrubs are best on their own and do not go well with the generally more rounded growth and soft mauves and purples of the older roses. Curve the edges of the beds if you have room to do this as it gives a less formal outline to the garden.

And now, finally, we come to a suggestion for a novelty bed. It will take some arranging to achieve balance of growth and colour unless you can do it on a really grand scale with groups of each variety placed together, for I am talking about a bed which will show the history of the rose. Start with one or two species, R. *foetida* of course, and maybe Canarybird or Stanwell Perpetual. R. *gallica officinalis*, the Red Rose of Lancaster or Rosa Mundi from the Gallicas, York and Lancaster and/or the Autumn Damask, *Alba semi-plena*, the White Rose of York or *alba maxima*, the Jacobite Rose of Bonnie Prince Charlie, R. *centifolia* itself for the Dutch Old Masters. Add any of the Moss Roses (perhaps Nuits de Young?), one Portland in Jacques Cartier, Slater's Crimson China, Souvenir de la Malmaison for Empress Josephine and the Bourbons, and Frau Karl Druschki for the Hybrid Perpetuals. Any Rugosa you like and any Hybrid Musk, though preferably one of the early ones raised by their originator, Joseph Pemberton. Any dated before about 1921 are likely to be his. Include a modern one or two if you have room and the inclination; Iceberg for the floribunda type or Fred Loads if you want gay colours, and Peace to represent a real landmark in Hybrid Teas. A real jumble sale, but it is an idea. I will leave you to find out whether or not it is a good one. I've hardly the space left for a single new rose planting in my own garden.

45

CHAPTER 4

Looking After Them

As a general statement which, like most general statements, needs some qualification later on, it can be said that most shrub roses do quite well on most kinds of soil. There are a number that really do need good soil and good cultivation and of course all of them will do better with extra care and attention. If they are not looked after, at the very least in their initial planting, they may not achieve their full potential in size, and vigour, the flowers may be smaller than they should be and less profuse, and they may lack their full beauty of colour and substance.

Shrub roses are long lived as a rule for they have the toughness of the species roses much closer behind them than the over-propagated Hybrid Teas and floribundas. They will under normal circumstances be in one spot for a long time, so it is essential to give them a well-prepared home. If you give them a good start, there is no reason why all the roses should not thrive on basically poor soil provided you take the trouble to make it better by feeding and mulching, but it might be useful to mention a few of the roses – and they include some of the best – that will be perfectly happy on dusty, sandy soil with the minimum of attention.

I have mentioned already that the Scotch Roses and the Rugosas come into this class. It would be interesting to plant a row of one of the Scotch species or near species close against a privet hedge and see which came off best, but it should be said that some of the Scotch hybrids like Frühlingsgold, Frühlingsmorgen, Frühlingsduft, Frühlingsanfang and Stanwell Perpetual need something a little better than the almost pure sand in which the true species will flourish, though they can cope with a pretty poverty-stricken diet.

The China Roses and the Hybrid Musks are other tough customers, as are some of the modern shrubs from Germany like

Elmshorn and Bonn, which have been bred very much with rugged conditions in mind. The Bourbon climber Zéphirine Drouhin, Canarybird and R. *moyesii* in its various forms and other modern shrubs like Lavender Lassie and Golden Wings also do well, though not all agree with me about the latter. Mr Graham Thomas (whom God preserve, just the same) has not found that it does well on sandy soil. The soil of my garden is as sandy as a day-tripper's sandwich and as dusty in the summer as the top of a wardrobe and my Golden Wings is six feet high, as much across, and still growing, with only a regular annual mulch of half-decayed leaves to help it. Another, which I grew from a cutting of the first, is about half the size of its parent in three years. So where does that get us? Buy Golden Wings anyway and feed it well if you find you have to. It is one of the very best of all single roses and always in bloom.

If you order your roses early, they should arrive in November, which is the best month for planting. The ground will still be reasonably warm, so that the roots can begin to grow and make themselves at home before the frosts and cold winter rains set in, and thus get under way more rapidly in the spring.

But do not wait for the roses to arrive before preparing the planting site.

Planting shrub roses is basically no different from planting any other rose – or other shrub for that matter – and ideally the ground should be prepared in September, about two months in advance. It is probably risky using the word "ideally", because one's immediate reaction is to say: "Well, no one is perfect," and to leave the digging of the holes until after the roses have come. I have done it myself, though fortunately on my light soil, which never compacts much anyway, it is probably not so vital to start early. On heavy, sticky soil it certainly is, to allow the soil surrounding the actual planting hole and into which the roots will spread to settle down again (though not as solidly as before, of course) and to begin the breaking down of the manure or compost you have worked into the lower level.

If you are planting a whole bed of shrub roses the whole bed should be dug over, yard by back-breaking yard, to twice the depth of the blade of your spade or about two feet. As much well-rotted manure as you can afford, or as much well-rotted compost as you can make, should be dug into the lower level.

Those two sentences cover a lot of work, but assuming you have persevered and not cancelled your rose order half-way through, you now have a breathing space of eight to ten weeks until the roses come. It may even be longer if you ordered late and they do not arrive until the spring. If this happens, there is no need to worry, for they can be planted safely at any time up to the end of March, or even April in the north of England and Scotland. They will be rather slower in getting away, but it is amazing how they will catch up.

During this rest period it might be a good idea to check over your planting plan if you have made one. Re-check the ultimate size of all the roses, making sure that they really will have room to grow (leaving a little less space for those that like to grow up through others) and that the tallest really are at the back or at the sides if it is a bed that you cannot walk right round. One of the most difficult things about planting shrubs is to visualise them

PLATE 5

Gallica roses	*page*
1. Alain Blanchard	75
2. Belle de Crécy	76
3. Camaieux	76
4. Cardinal de Richelieu	77
5. Charles de Mills	78
6. Empress Josephine	78
7. Jenny Duval	78
8. Officinalis	78
9. Rosa Mundi	78

```
1   2   3

4   5   6

7   8   9
```

fully grown and to allow enough space for them. With slow-growing shrubs you can fill in the vast open spaces in between with annuals, or temporarily with comparatively short-lived quick starters like some of the brooms, but fortunately roses do grow quickly themselves and the acres of bare earth will vanish after two seasons at the most.

Do not forget, too, that if you have chosen roses that spread by suckering, that they *will* spread by suckering and allowance must be made. You cannot ignore this and hope for the best as the suckers will not be too easy to get at when the roses bush out and grow together and you will, in effect, have planted them too closely so that they may tend to smother each other.

If you are planting only one or two specimen shrubs, or introducing individuals into an existing shrub border, you should still dig the ground where they are to grow in the same way and add compost and/or manure. The hole should be at least three feet across and again two spade blades deep, with the bottom soil well broken up. In light soil particularly, to help it to hold water, it is

1	**2**	**3**
4	**5**	**6**
7	**8**	**9**

PLATE 6

Gallica roses   page

1. Surpasse Tout   79
2. Tricolore de Flandre   79
3. Tuscany Superb   79

Damask roses

4. Blush Damask   80
5. Celsiana   80
6. Mme Hardy   81
7. Quartre Saisons   81
8. St Nicholas   81
9. York and Lancaster   81

a good idea to put some old turves, grass side downwards, at the bottom of the hole. These will rot down gradually and add humus. Fill in the hole and once more you wait for the rose or roses.

I have already suggested that a square or circle cut for a specimen in a lawn should just about equal the spread of the fully-grown rose, but self-preservation is not the only reason for doing this. It will mean in addition that the roots of the rose will have no competition from the roots of the grass, rain can penetrate easily, there is somewhere for the mulch to go (though the blackbirds and thrushes will not leave it there long), and you will not have the horrible job of trying to keep the grass which the mower cannot reach tidy.

When planting climbers against a wall, especially that of a house, dig your planting hole at the very least eighteen inches away from the brickwork. You can slant the rose in towards the wall when you plant it, but the soil close in will always be very dry, especially so if the house has large, overhanging eaves. In other words, put your rose where the rain can get at the roots.

Much the same sort of thing applies when planting a climber that is to ramble through a tree. Keep the hole a reasonable distance away from the trunk to give the sun and rain a chance of reaching the rose and where, incidentally, you are less likely to come up against a barrier of thick tree roots with your spade. Choose the windward side of your tree so that the trailing branches of the climber will be blown naturally into the tree as they grow. They will have to be tied in and trained at first, but after that you can let them, within reason, take their own course. Do not choose a rose that must have annual pruning unless you make a hobby of self-pity.

If you are going to plant a rose hedge it is much better (and easier) to dig a trench about two feet deep where the hedge is to run rather than to make a series of individual planting holes. Work your manure into the bottom of the trench, the width of which will depend on whether you are planting the roses in a single line or staggering them. For a single line, three feet wide should be ample. Staggering will produce a thicker hedge, but most shrub roses are big and bushy enough for this not to be needed.

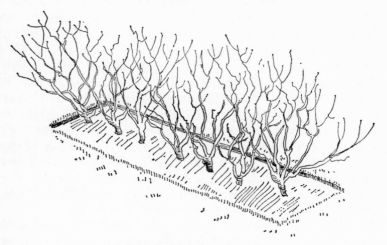

Planting a rose hedge

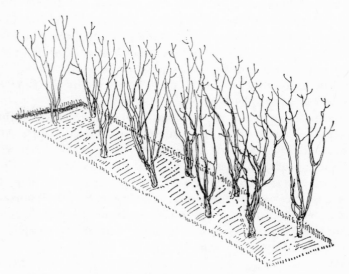

Staggered planting for upright trees

The general planting distance given for hedges is about three to four feet apart, but obviously this must vary according to the habit of growth of your roses. I would suggest that their distance apart should be half their final spread, which I have found to work very well. It covers you for very upright growers like Queen Elizabeth (which is one that does benefit from staggering), and equally well for the wide-spreading Hybrid Musks. If your rose hedge is replacing another hedge, which will be likely to have taken most of the good out of the ground, you should, I am afraid, replace the soil entirely, taking it from another part of the garden which has not grown roses. This latter point is important, as one should never plant a new rose in soil where another rose has grown. Always replace the soil, as it will have become "rose sick" and the new rose will never do well.

For a really high hedge, using something like Conrad Ferdinand Meyer or any of the climbers or ramblers, some support is really essential. For this, oak posts about six to eight feet apart are best, with four or five equally-spaced strands of strong galvanised wire strung between them. Climbers should be planted about fifteen inches apart and the canes trained out in a fan shape, keeping them as horizontal as possible so that all the flowers do not come at the top, with only bare stems lower down. If you are going to use posts and wires, put the posts in when you dig your trench in September so that they are firmly set by the time you come to the actual planting.

An alternative to the use of wires is to adopt a scheme which you can see used with great success in Queen Mary's Rose Gardens at Regent's Park in London. There a very stout rope links the top of each post with the next one, not stretched tight, but dipping in the middle. The roses are trained first of all up the posts and then along the ropes, meeting each other mid-way between each post. The result is very beautiful, but it is not strictly speaking a hedge, and it does need plenty of space to carry it out effectively.

Suckers in a hedge can be a headache, firstly because it is not always easy to spot them, and secondly because, once the hedge has thickened up, even Brer Rabbit would hesitate about volunteering to get them out. Planting roses on their own roots will

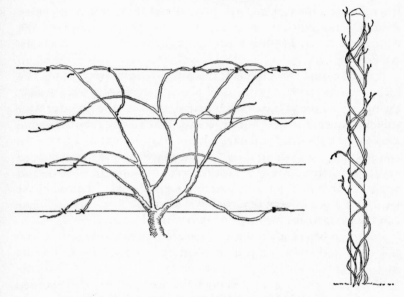

Training a rambler or climber on a wall or fence
Training a rose on a pillar by winding stems round in a spiral

prevent you getting suckers of a different rose, but unless you
grow them this way yourself from cuttings, which would be
quite a big undertaking for a big hedge, you would be likely to
have difficulty in getting the rose you want grown in this way
from a nursery, except as a special order, and it might with some
roses produce a less vigorous hedge. All in all it is not a problem
I can provide an answer for, except to say that I have never had
a Hybrid Musk that suckered. Rather deeper planting than usual
of some of the Gallicas, like Rosa Mundi, should cause them to
sucker from the rose itself and not the rootstock. This will help
to build the hedge up more quickly and increase its spread, which
with these comparatively small roses is an advantage rather than
a drawback.

All these words and the roses haven't even come yet. Well, they
will arrive eventually and the nursery will have packed them so
that, if it is frosty at the time or the ground is wet and waterlogged,
or you are just too busy to deal with them, they can be safely left

for up to ten days or so, still packed and in a cool, frost-proof shed. Do not store them in a warm atmosphere. They will not thank you for it. English roses, naturally, like to sleep with the window open.

It is, of course, best to plant the roses straight away, but if you really cannot carry out your final planting even after the ten days are up, you must at least snatch half an hour on the first day with suitable weather to heel your roses in. This simply means digging a hole – or a trench if you have a lot of bushes – about a foot deep and putting the roses in it so that they have at least six inches of soil over their roots. If you can soak the roots in a bucket of water for about an hour first, all to the good, and if the soil in the trench or hole is very dry, water it after the roses are in. They can then be left for a month or two if need be.

But to go back for a minute to the actual unpacking, which you will have to do whether you are planting straight away or heeling in.

Once the packing is removed, inspect the plants carefully. First check the labels to make sure that you have got what you ordered – assuming that the labels are correct, of course, though even the best of nurseries can slip up occasionally. See that the plants are healthy looking, with firm smooth wood and well developed root growth. There are minimum standards laid down by the BSI for first grade bushes, but I am not sure that they can be applied in all cases to shrub roses because their habit of growth varies so much. It should, however, not be difficult to see whether or not you have got a sickly-looking plant or one that is badly damaged or has poor roots. The neck of the root-stock should be at least five-eighths of an inch thick and there should be plenty of fibrous roots.

If you have got a bad rose, return it at once to the nursery, which is almost certain to replace it if your complaint is justified and you are dealing with a good firm. If there are any leaves still on the plant, cut them off, leaving the leaf stalks. Pulling off may encourage entry of disease if the bark is torn. Finally check that there are no suckers growing from the roots. These should have been removed before the roses were dispatched, but one or two may have been missed. Any reasonably substantial growth with a

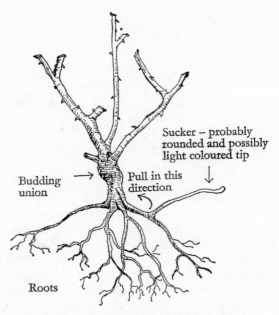

Sucker – probably
rounded and possibly
light coloured tip

Budding
union

Pull in this
direction

Roots

Removing sucker from a newly bought rose

green or whitish tip coming from below the point where the top
growth starts is likely to be a sucker and should be pulled off.
Do not simply snip them away with secateurs or you will leave
dormant sucker buds behind. And do not pull away any suckers
if the plants are on their own roots.

If all is well, and nine times out of ten it will be for I have been
describing the worst that could happen, put the roses in a bucket
(or buckets) of water, making sure that all the roots are submerged.
They can stay there while you dig your heeling-in trench or
planting holes, but not, as I said earlier, for less than an hour and
preferably for longer.

For the actual planting you will need, apart from a spade, a
bucket or more of planting mixture to help with quick rooting,
particularly if your soil is on the heavy side. This mixture is
simply equal parts of fine soil and fine-grade peat, well mixed up
and with two or three handfuls of bone meal or hoof and horn

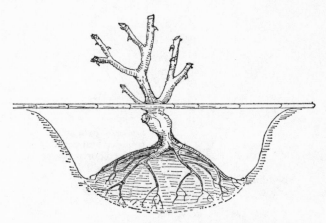

Using a cane to show correct depth for planting

meal added and well stirred in as well. You can carry your roses to the planting site in the bucket or else you should have some damp sacking to wrap the roots in to prevent them drying out, especially if the day is a windy one. If you are planting Rugosas or any of the Scotch Rose hybrids, you will also need a pair of strong, thorn-proof gloves, though if a thorn has your name on it – .

Dig your planting holes wide enough to allow the roots of the roses to be well spread out, which is most important, not only so that they can absorb the maximum amount of food, but also so that they can anchor the bush. The holes should be deep enough to allow the budding union to be just below soil level and a bamboo cane placed across the hole after the rose has been put into it will help you to judge this. If you like to dig the hole rather deeper and put in an extra helping of manure or compost at the bottom it can do nothing but good, provided that it is covered with at least three inches of soil before the rose goes in. Direct contact between the roots and manure could burn them.

Finally, before you actually plant the rose, trim with your secateurs to about two-thirds of their length any long, thick roots, as this will encourage the fine feeding roots to grow from them and establish the rose more quickly.

The counsel of perfection, the counsel in fact given by the

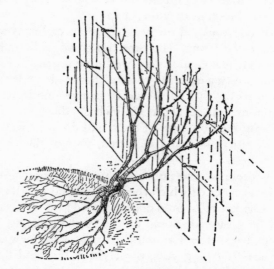

Fanning out roots of a climber away from wall

Royal National Rose Society in their handbook *The Cultivation of the Rose*, is to heap the soil up a little in the middle of the planting hole and spread the roots out evenly all round. Fine if you have evenly distributed roots, but what rose has? In real life, getting the roots to go where you want them to is like trying to put a reluctant cat into a cat basket. So? Spread them out as well as you can without damaging or straining any of them, hold the rose in position in the hole with one hand, and put several hand-fuls of the planting mixture over the roots. Pull in some earth from the surrounding bed as well, and as soon as the roots are well covered, tread it down gently but firmly. Pull in more earth until the hole is all but filled and tread again. For my kind of sandy soil I add a little more compost at this stage, keeping it clear of the stems, and then top up with still more earth to just above bed level to allow for a little settling. All that remains is two gallons of water for the rose and a Scotch per rose (up to four bushes) for yourself. Tread in lightly again after a day or two and again after a hard frost. That's it.

Climbers against a wall should have their roots fanned outwards away from it, rather than spread out all round. They will then be pointed in the direction they ought to go.

I have already touched on pruning in an earlier chapter in a very general sort of way. The time has come to be rather more specific, though one cannot very well give a general instruction about pruning such a diverse group as that made up by the shrub roses, except to say that all should be pruned moderately hard – to three or four eyes or about six inches – the first spring after planting. From then on most of them will do quite well with the minimum of attention that I indicated, though they will not be at their very best.

Inevitably there are exceptions to this. R. *banksiae lutea*, and the other Banksian roses of which there are several besides the one I describe in Chapter 16, should not be pruned at all or the flowering stems will be removed. Some of the once-flowering kinds do better if cut back after blooming to encourage new flowering shoots for the following year, the Hybrid Teas and floribundas used as shrubs should be pruned as for other strong-growing roses of the same sort, and some of the Rugosas and Gallicas can be clipped lightly with shears. There are, as you can see, a lot of different answers and to stop both of us ending up as confused as the hawthorn tree must have been when it first learned that it was a member of the same family as the rose, I will cover the detailed pruning instructions under the various group headings, and where necessary under a single variety in the chapters that follow immediately after this one.

There are just one or two more general points that could be made. The first is, do not overdo the pruning.

If a rose grows naturally to six feet in height and as much across, let it do so as nearly as possible. You can do some shaping and remove the odd truant branch that wanders out across a path, but if you try to confine it to three feet tall just because you have not left sufficient room for it, you cannot expect it to have its natural beauty of form or full quota of bloom. Rose hedges are rather different, for in effect when you prune them you are shaping one gigantic plant and not a series, so that the shape of the *individuals* is not so important. Do not, however, get a six-foot rose for a three foot hedge unless you are certain that it will stand the treatment, though it would be rather pointless even then.

Finally, one is generally told to prune a Hybrid Tea or floribunda just above an outward facing bud to keep the bush open. With the widely varying habits of growth in shrub roses, this rule cannot always be applied. Prune just above a bud which is pointing in the direction you want a new growth to develop, which in some cases will be outwards, but may well be upwards on an arching cane.

Hedges should have selected strong growths cut hard back to near the base every other year to encourage flowering laterals low down and prevent the base becoming bare, though with a really tangled, vigorous hedge this is much easier to say than to do.

It is interesting to note that late nineteenth-century writers, including that great gardener Gertude Jekyll in her book *The Rose Garden* – and remember that the roses they were growing and writing about were all what we now call shrub roses – do not deal with or even mention black spot, though they all tell you how to treat mildew and rust. The Persian rose, R. *foetida*, which was introduced into the rose breeding lines about the turn of the century, is popularly supposed to have passed on its passion for the black spot to all the roses which have descended from it, which means a very large proportion of our modern varieties. I have never, however, seen any reference to it being the originator of the disease, and it is held by some that it never had black spot itself in its native land, but merely succumbed when it came in contact with it on others because it had no in-built resistance. I am not sure that anyone knows the answer to this one. Perhaps the Victorians did not recognise it as a disease, though if they lived in the pure air of the west country it would be difficult to believe this could be so.

There are certainly shrub roses other than the Persian Yellow that can get black spot, just as a number of them can be infected by mildew and a few by rust. The old roses are tough and seem to be able to shrug off attacks more readily than modern varieties, but of course they can pass them on to the other roses and can become unsightly themselves, so spray straight away if there is any sign of disease. If not, leave them alone.

Try to wet the whole plant when you spray as the under sides of the leaves are just as important as the tops and you will really have a sense of achievement if you manage this with an eight foot by eight foot bush. There are several excellent rose fungicides on the market – I use Murphy's myself – all easy to use and safe if you follow the maker's instructions. The modern pressure sprayers with plastic pressure-chambers-cum-spray-containers are a joy to use (if anything about spraying can be a joy), and are sufficiently powerful to penetrate even very tangled growth.

The same general pattern should be followed when spraying against insect pests like greenfly. I have never seen them on some shrub roses, notably the Rugosa family, many of which are practically disease-proof as well, but not all are equally immune. So watch for attack by greenfly and other pests and if it comes, spray at once with a systemic insecticide which will last for weeks and not be washed off by the rain, as it enters the sap of the plant. If there are no pests, do not spray. Apart from the hard work, it is not cheap.

Discounting pruning and occasional spraying there is very little routine maintenance needed for shrub roses. A handful of bonemeal or powdered rose fertiliser scattered round but not on each plant and then lightly hoed in, after pruning and again in July, will do a lot of good. So will an annual mulching with manure or compost in April. This will feed the soil, help it to keep moist, which it must be already when you put the mulch on, and it will keep the weeds down. If you have a group of shrubs growing sufficiently closely to prevent them being blown all over the lawn, rake some of your leaves in amongst them when they fall from the trees in the autumn, spreading them evenly two or three inches thick. They will have rotted down by the following autumn into the most wonderful leaf-mould and there will not be a weed in sight amongst the shrubs. Any lilies and other tall-growing plants you may have planted will push up quite happily through the leaves in the spring. Keep the leaves away from the edges of the beds, for blackbirds and thrushes looking for insects will scatter them back on to the lawn just as effectively and much more persistently than the wind.

It is a routine with all roses to look for suckers, but with the shrub roses that are close to species themselves it is likely to be more difficult to recognise them than it is with Hybrid Teas and floribundas. The rootstocks, also being species or near species, may have leaves and growth very similar to the shrub. If a shoot comes up some way from the bush it is almost certain to be a sucker, but the only sure way of tracking one down with any kind of rose is to trace it back to where it joins the bush by gently scraping away some of the soil. If it comes from below the budding union it is a sucker, and should be pulled away, just as you treated the suckers on the newly-arrived plants. An awkward one may come from right under the bush, or from the middle of a tough tangle of roots, in which case proper removal will be difficult, but do the best you can, short of pulling the whole rose out of the ground. And once again, never cut a sucker off at ground level. You will simply have pruned it and encouraged even more energetic growth.

Continuous flowering or repeat flowering shrub roses should have old flower heads or heps removed if you want a really good second showing. The Hybrid Musks, the Hybrid Perpetuals and the Rugosas come into this category. You need not, however, remove those of once flowering varieties and of course with many of them, like the Moyesii family, the heps in the autumn are part of their display. On the other hand the single-flowered Rugosas and some other roses have both a continuous flower display and heps as well, so in this case remove the old flowers only after the first main flush of bloom in June and July. The second flush will give you heps aplenty.

CHAPTER 5

The Species Roses

THE roses described in the following chapters represent only a small selection of the shrub roses which you can grow. They are, however, representative of all the main groups and are some of the best for general garden use for all types and sizes of gardens. Only in one or two cases, for example the York and Lancaster Rose and Souvenir de la Malmaison, have I included roses that are not of the front rank for the garden, but they have a place in an old rose collection because of their historical associations. Buy them if you have plenty of room, but not otherwise.

All the roses listed can be obtained without too much difficulty. You will not get any of them in supermarkets and chain stores, though I have, for the first time, seen one of the best known, the Bourbon climber, Zéphirine Drouhin, sold as a pre-packed rose in a specialist garden shop, which is perhaps a sign of things to come. However, an increasing number of general nurseries and specialist rose growers are including at least a few, and sometimes quite a large number, in their lists. A selection of the growers that do carry a wide range is listed in Chapter 17.

Where they have been awarded, I have shown the Royal Horticultural Society Award of Merit (AM), and the even better Award of Garden Merit (AGM), and First Class Certificate (FCC) and also the awards of Trial Ground Certificates (TGC), Certificates of Merit (CofM) and Gold Medals (GM), by the Royal National Rose Society. These awards mean that the roses which have won them are very good, but it does not mean, in the case of the old shrub roses, that those that have no award are necessarily not so good. They may be even better, but the roses of the periods we are dealing with were not submitted for awards as regularly as they are nowadays. Many of the best date from long before the award era and have never even tried to get one, though a grower can still submit an old rose if he wishes. This explains why some of the dates of the awards bear little relation to the date of introduction of the rose.

And while we are on the subject of dates of introduction, it might be worth explaining why some roses in an otherwise ancient category bear quite a recent date. An example of this is the Damask Rose, St Nicholas, which was only discovered growing in a Yorkshire garden in 1950, though it is obviously very much older than that. There are others in the same class.

One important group of roses I have intentionally left out altogether and that is the Tea Roses. This is because they are only hardy enough to grow out of doors in a very few parts of the country. The only Tea I have included is a climbing one, Gloire de Dijon, which some think has a hardier rose somewhere in its ancestry, and which will, in any case, usually have the shelter of a wall or fence.

The ultimate height and spread of each bush in my list is given (height first), but this must be taken as a rough guide only. It gives a good average, but dimensions can vary greatly with soil, cultivation, and the position in which the rose is grown.

THE SPECIES

I have already indicated that the majority of species are probably too big for a small garden. If you have space for a large lilac you could put most of the species in its place, but why not choose a shrub rose that will flower twice instead? If, however, you really want one, some that flower over quite a long period and have attractive ferny foliage for the rest of the year are Canarybird, R. *cantabrigiensis*, R. *ecae*, R. *moyesii* Highdownensis, R. *multibracteata*, R. *soulieana* and R. *webbiana*. Some that have attractive and spectacular heps from about August onwards include R. *forrestiana*, R. *moyesii* itself and its hybrids Eos and Geranium, and R. *pomifera duplex*. R. *rubrifolia* can be grown for its unusual purple-tinted foliage and rather less showy heps (its flowers are nothing to get excited about) and R. *sericea pteracantha* for its remarkable translucent red thorns.

A few do flower more than once, as you may remember. These

are Nevada, Marguerite Hilling, Frühlingsmorgen and Stanwell Perpetual.

For a small garden I would not be without at least one of the following if I was going to have a species at all: Canarybird grown as a standard, R. *ecae*, which is tallish but not too spreading, R. *rubrifolia*, which can get quite big but is not a dense grower, Ormiston Roy if you have a difficult, dry area to cope with, and/or Stanwell Perpetual.

For a medium or large garden, the choice is wide open. All those listed are worth growing. Pruning consists of cutting out old, spent wood every year or two and tipping back after flowering over-eager branches that may get out of control – allowing for the fact that you may be cutting off the heps as well.

Canarybird: Comes from Northern China and Korea. Sometimes listed as R. *xanthina spontanea* which is a different variety, though probably a close relative. 6–7ft by 7ft when grown as a bush. I have two standards, eight years old and with 1½in diameter stems which are even taller but only spread about 4–5ft. It may start flowering in April in a good year, but will certainly do so in May, the flowers lasting fully three weeks, with sometimes an odd one or two later at the tips of the shoots. The rounded bush with its

PLATE 7

Alba roses   *page*

1. *alba maxima*   84
2. *alba semi-plena*   84
3. Belle Amour   85
4. Celestial (Céleste)   85
5. Felicite Parmentier   86
6. Koenigin von Danemarck   86
7. Mme Plantier   86
8. Great Maiden's Blush   86
9. Maiden's Blush   87

1	2	3
4	5	6
7	8	9

attractive ferny foliage, has each of its long, arching shoots literally smothered with its 2in, bright yellow, lightly scented, single flowers, in my garden the first of all to open in the Spring, and all the lovelier for that. Each flower is on a very short stalk arising from a leaf axil so that they nestle into the leaves. Said to be subject to die-back. I have not found this, though I have never grown it as a bush, which may make some difference. Does not mind poor soil, but does like full sun. It will occasionally send up a shoot much more vigorous than the rest. This can be left, or it can be cut back after flowering by about a half, when it will send out arching shoots of its own, forming as it were a second tier to the cake.

R. *cantabrigiensis*: 1931. Another early flowering yellow and a better, more vigorous and upright offspring of one that is much better known and probably more often listed, R. *hugonis*. 7ft by 7ft, the arching branches are covered in May and into June with creamy-yellow, semi-double, 2in blooms amongst the fern-like leaves. Not as arching in growth as Canarybird, but it does have small round orange heps in late summer, which the latter does not. Hardly any thorns and a sweet fragrance. AM 1931.

R. *complicata*: Probably a hybrid with a Gallica rose, this is not

PLATE 8

such a tall one (5ft), but it will either spread out to about 8ft or else clamber through hedges and over low walls or into the lower branches of a tree. It has very large and very beautiful single flowers of a brilliant pink with a white eye and yellow stamens. I have seen them described as being as large as saucers, which in my experience is something of an exaggeration unless one was thinking of a very dainty coffee set. They appear all along the arching shoots amid the large, light green, smooth, pointed foliage. AM 1951. FCC 1958.

R. *dupontii*: Earlier than 1817. Another Gallica hybrid, this time with the Musk Rose. 7ft by 7ft, it blooms at midsummer in June and July with its flowers in clusters. They are large, up to 3in, a mixture of blush-white and cream and there is a rich musk fragrance, which is to be expected with the family history. The stamens are golden. It can be grown as a free, lax bush or as a short climber or pillar rose to about 8ft. It is generally healthy and the flowers do not fade as do those of many roses of such delicate colouring. Weather resistance is good.

R. *ecae*: From Afghanistan in 1880, though early writers, including Gertrude Jekyll, described it as coming from Abyssinia. Another early bloomer, starting in May to display its bright yellow, 1in, single flowers, which have the intense colour of a buttercup. The bush will go to 5ft and sometimes rather more, by about 4ft wide. The canes are thin and wiry, reddish brown and attractive, with tiny leaves. AM 1933.

R. *foetida bicolor*: Sometimes listed, though I have been unable to discover the reason, as the Austrian Copper. Prior to 1590. It comes from Asia Minor and the Middle East and is a sport from its yellow parent, R. *foetida*. It makes as a rule a not terribly vigorous 5ft by 4ft rather spindly shrub which, in June and July, has the most vividly coloured flowers of all wild roses. About $1\frac{1}{4}$in in diameter and single, they come on short stems on the old wood and frequently on the ends of the branches. They are of a flaming orange-red, with a yellow reverse to the petals and with the peculiar, heavy scent which gave its name to the *foetida* family. It is best grown with some protection, preferably on a wall, where it will flower freely provided it has sun as well, though strangely, considering its place of origin, it seems to do best in the cooler districts of this country. It needs rich deep soil to give of its best, is slow to establish, and resents any but the lightest of pruning. Occasionally the odd branch will sport back to its yellow parent. Keep a sharp lookout for black spot. Despite its drawbacks, an exciting shrub to have around.

R. *foetida persiana*: 1847 and also known as the Persian Yellow. The flowers are very double and of the most intense yellow, but otherwise this rose is a duplicate of R. *foetida bicolor*. This is the one that gave us our modern yellow roses and *bicolor* gave us our flames and present day bicolors.

R. *forrestiana*: From western China. This forms eventually a very large 7ft shrub, spreading out almost as far, but it is slow to establish and slow growing. The growths are long and arching and bear in June and July smallish single, carmine-pink flowers, which have a white eye and pale yellow stamens. They come in clusters on short stalks, surrounded by the most unusual leafy bracts, which in due course frame the small, signal-red heps in the autumn. The plum-red new wood is attractive. Not a showy shrub, but an interesting one. AM 1956.

R. *hugonis headleyensis*: About 1920. Another and even more beautiful and even larger (9ft by 12ft) seedling form of the early-flowering single yellow, R. *hugonis*. It is very fragrant and the medium-sized flowers are of a soft creamy yellow all along the widely sweeping, delicate branches. They are not unlike large primroses. For large gardens only, where the sight of a bush in full bloom in early June will not be forgotten – ever.

R. *macrantha*: 1823. One of the sprawlers or, more kindly, a trailing rose. Only about 5ft high, it will reach out in all directions to 9 or 10ft, with its lax canes studded with 4in single, blush-pink or almost white flowers with golden stamens. They come in small clusters, have a sweet scent, and are followed by ¾in round red heps. For the low foreground of a shrubbery or for running wild over banks. June–July.

R. *macrantha* 'Lady Curzon': A 1901 hybrid with a Rugosa that does not much resemble either parent, it forms a great 8ft by 8ft rounded, tangled bush, which will scramble into a tree if given the chance. It flowers from mid- to late June only, when it is covered with the most marvellous single, pink, 4in flowers with creamy stamens and curiously wrinkled petals. Another good *macrantha* hybrid is blush-pink Daisy Hill.

R. *moyesii*: From Western China in 1894. The famous gardener William Robinson, writing in a late edition of his *The English Flower Garden*, said: "Men talk of getting fine things by crossing this, but they will never get anything so good." Well he was certainly right, at least as far as the larger garden is concerned, for it will grow up to 12ft in height and 10ft across, erect but not very full at the bottom, giving the effect of an inverted triangle. It flowers in late May and June – sometimes running over into July – when it is a mass of brilliant crimson-red, single 2½–3in flowers with creamy stamens setting them off to perfection, one or two blooms on each short spur along the gently arching branches. It has small, elegant foliage and is not too dense a grower, so that it is a good companion for plants that need partial shade. There is little if any scent – opinions are divided about this, but I have never detected any – but from August onwards come the most

PLATE 9

Moss roses   page

1. Capitaine John Ingram   91
2. Duchess de Verneuil   92
3. Général Kleber   92
4. Gloire de Mousseux   92
5. Henri Martin   93
6. Jeanne de Montfort   179
7. Nuits de Young   94
8. William Lobb   94

1	2	3
4		5
6	7	8

striking bottle-shaped heps, though here again I could say that for a time I was prepared to dispute this as well. For two years mine had not a hep in sight until I put a handful of sulphate of potash round each bush in early spring. That cured the trouble, which was obviously due to a soil deficiency. If you have the same problem, try this and see, though strangely I have not had the same difficulties with the heps of other roses growing nearby. AM 1908, AGM 1925, FCC 1916.

R. *moyesii* 'Eos': A comparatively modern *moyesii* hybrid dating from 1950, it has semi-double blooms of a vivid coral-red, but no heps afterwards. Generally similar to R. *moyesii* in growth, about 12ft high by 7ft across, the arching growths are a soft coral-red – not as bright as the flowers but a similar tone – when young. Little scent.

R. *moyesii* 'Geranium': 1938. 10ft by 8ft and the best of this family for the smaller garden, though it is still hardly a dwarf. It flowers in early June, the blooms being of a slightly lighter red than R. *moyesii*, but still very striking with their cream stamens, though they, too, have little scent. Rather more foliage and more compact growth than its parent. The heps if anything are bigger.

1	**2**	**3**
4	**5**	**6**
		10
7	**8**	**9**

PLATE 10

China roses	*page*
1. Bloomfield Abundance	95
2. Cecile Brunner	95
3. Little White Pet	96
4. Natalie Nypels	96
5. Perle d'Or	96
6. Hermosa	180
7. Slater's Crimson China	97
8. *viridiflora*	97

Portland roses	
9. Comte de Chambord	98
10. Jacques Cartier	98

R. *moyesii* 'Highdownensis': Dating from 1928, this is another big one, reaching 10ft and as much across. It has the small, dainty leaves of the type, rather glaucous on the under sides, and the arching stems are a rich, reddish brown. The flowers appear in early June and are some 2½in across, single and of a deep pink with buff anthers and little if any perfume. Large, brilliant scarlet heps of the usual *moyesii* elongated bottle shape. AM 1928.

R. *moyesii* 'Nevada': 1927. A *moyesii* crossed with an HT and recurrent in bloom as a result. This is one of the most magnificent of all garden shrubs and also one of the largest, growing to 7ft by 7ft or more as a fairly dense, arching bush. The reddish-brown stems have few thorns and the foliage is abundant, quite small and light green and not, unfortunately, quite proof against black spot. But the real glory is in the flowers, which are semi-double, about 3½in across, and of a very pale creamy white, sometimes slightly flushed with pink. They come on the short side shoots of the old wood and also in clusters at the ends of growth of the current year, and in such profusion that the whole bush is almost completely hidden by them. Its main flush is in May and June and it will then flower intermittently until the second, slightly less prolific blooming in August and September, with a few more flowers to come even after that. Only slight scent. No heps. AM 1949. FCC 1954.

R. *moyesii* 'Marguerite Hilling': 1959. A deep pink sport of Nevada and similar in every way except its colouring. I have found it a slower starter, but I have not heard of anyone else with the same experience and it may simply be that the siting of mine is not ideal for it. AM 1960.

R. *multibracteata*: From Western China in 1910, this is a huge, very prickly shrub with tiny, greyish-green leaves which are scented like the Sweet Brier. The 1in, single, rosy-lilac flowers, which are also scented, are produced in great profusion all over the bush in July, lasting for about three weeks with a few intermittently afterwards in August. They occur all along the arching shoots, which generally terminate in a large, many-flowered cluster. Small, hairy heps. An interesting rose in recent breeding history as it was one of the parents of Floradora which, in turn, produced Montezuma and Queen Elizabeth, the first of the very tall-growing floribundas known, at least in America where they originated, as Grandifloras.

R. *paulii rosea*: Like R. *macrantha* a sprawling spreader, only 3ft high but covering the ground for 10ft or more around and rooting as it goes. The flowers are single and of a soft pink, rather like clematis blooms, and are surrounded by pale green bracts. The stamens are yellow and there is a rich scent. Flowering time is June/July and if it is planted where it can hang down over a wall or steep bank it will form a 15ft waterfall of blossom. R. *paulii* is similar but white.

R. *pomifera duplex*: Also known as R. *villosa* and as Wolley Dod's Rose after the Rev. Wolley Dod, who first grew it in his garden. It comes from Europe and Western Asia. It forms a 7ft by 7ft bush flowering in May and June with 2in semi-double pink blooms coming from carmine buds. The leaves are soft grey-green and downy. In late summer the flowers are followed by very large and hairy, rounded, crimson heps. AM 1954.

R. *rubiginosa*: Also known as the Sweet Brier, Eglantine or R. *eglanteria* and at 8ft by 8ft it needs plenty of room. The flowers are single, pink, and rather fleeting and there are small, oval red heps in the autumn, but the unusual feature of this rose is its strongly aromatic foliage, the scent of which will spread for yards around on a damp summer evening. It grows into a great old tangle and will, though I do not myself recommend it, form an enormous and quite impenetrable hedge if the bushes are planted about 4–5ft apart. To keep this under some sort of control, remove the old wood if you can get at it, shorten all shoots that have flowered and also the most unruly of the long, whip-like canes in spring.

R. *rubiginosa*'s chief claim to distinction in my mind is as the dominant parent in the crosses that produced the Penzance Briers, a selection of which follows. Generally speaking their habit of growth is similar, though they are not all as robust. All have the same scented foliage.

R. *rubiginosa* 'Amy Robsart': 1894. Rich pink flowers, semi-double, in early June, and scarlet heps in the autumn. 8ft by 8ft. AM 1853.

R. *rubiginosa* 'Meg Merrilees': About the same size as Amy Robsart, but with crimson, single, scented flowers. 1894.

R. *rubiginosa* 'Lady Penzance': 1894. Possibly the best flowers of all the Penzance roses and only 6ft by 6ft. Single, yellowish-copper flowers in early June reflect its other parent, R. *foetida*, which also means that black spot is likely, though the same is true of the other Penzance hybrids. AM 1891.

R. *rubiginosa* 'Lord Penzance': 1894. A more vigorous grower than Lady Penzance, but again only up to about 6ft. Flowers single and of a fawny yellow. Scented. FCC 1890.

R. *rubrifolia*: From central and eastern Europe prior to 1830, this forms a fairly large (6ft by 6ft), open bush, almost without thorns. The small, purplish-pink flowers in June are not showy, though they produce clusters of attractive pinkish heps in the autumn. It is the colouring of the rest of the bush that makes it so well worth growing. The long, thin canes (completely thornless when young) have reddish-brown bark and the leaves are a most unusual grey-green with a purple, plum-like sheen. The colour intensifies and becomes even more purple if the bushes are in slight shade. It is growing quite happily against a north wall in a friend's garden, though it has not reached its full stature. AM (for fruit) 1949.

R. *sericea pteracantha*: Flowers nearly as soon as Canarybird in May and the single transient blooms are small, white, and have four petals instead of the usual five, which is distinction enough for any rose. But there is more to come. It forms a very vigorous, impenetrable shrub, often as much as 10ft by 10ft, the rather horizontal branches bearing huge thorns, flattened and enlarged at the base and continuing along the branches in almost unbroken lines. On the young shoots they are of a translucent red and extremely striking with the sun shining through them. They become very hard and sharp when mature. You can prune the bush quite hard to obtain the new shoots for use in the house. From Western China.

R. *soulieana*: Yet another shrub rose from Western China, about 1837, and another large bush, 10ft by 10ft, of arching, rather sprawling habit, mounding itself up gradually. The small leaves are an attractive silver grey-green, and set off to perfection the hundreds of single white flowers that open from yellow buds and have a yellow centre and stamens. They come in large, branching clusters in June and have a sweet scent.

R. *spinosissima* 'Ormiston Roy': The *spinosissimas* are the Scotch or Burnet Roses and this and the five to follow are some of their hybrids. Ormiston Roy originated in 1938, and is a 4ft, sturdy, bushy shrub which flowers early and is ideal for a small garden. It has single, deep yellow flowers, the petals veined darker, with ¾in blackish-maroon heps to follow, which have been likened to large black currants.

R. *spinosissima* 'Frühlingsanfang': Produced in 1950, this is one of the famous Frühlings group of roses produced in Germany by Wilhelm Kordes, using R. *spinosissima* as one parent, much as Lord Penzance produced the Penzance Briers, but with much better results as garden shrubs. Frühlingsanfang has large, single, ivory white flowers in early June, which grow all along the arching branches and are very fragrant. They are followed by maroon-red heps amongst the dark green foliage, which assumes autumn tints as it ages. Up to 8ft by 8ft.

R. *spinosissima* 'Frühlingsgold': Sometimes listed under the translation of its name, Spring Gold, this was first introduced in 1937. It is enormously vigorous, quickly reaching 8–9ft with huge arching branches many feet long taking it out to about the same width. Each branch in late May and early June is laden down with enormous 4–5in creamy-yellow semi-double flowers, which open wide but in which some of the petals in-curve. The stamens are amber and the scent is glorious. Its pointed, medium-green leaves are quite disease-proof, though in some seasons they seem to find great favour with the leaf-rolling sawfly. A great rose, fully deserving its AM 1950, AGM 1965 and FCC 1955.

R. *spinosissima* 'Frühlingsmorgen': 1941. This one has a great advantage in that it is recurrent, with another crop of flowers in

September after the first May/June flush. The 4in single blooms are of extreme beauty, of a soft pink shading to yellow in the centre and with maroon stamens, though they can fade almost to white after a time. Not such a strong grower as Frühlingsgold, it will reach 6ft by about 5–6ft, with smallish, matt, medium-green leaves. Strong fragrance. AM 1951.

R. *spinosissima* 'Frühlingsduft': 1949. Interesting in that it results from a cross between R. *spinosissima* and the same Hybrid Tea as Frühlingsanfang. In the latter case the result took more after the species and here the flowers, though not the shrub, take after the HT. They are creamy-apricot in colouring, double and with the scrolled buds of the HT. Richly scented, they come on a 6ft by 6ft bush in early June.

R. *spinosissima* 'Stanwell Perpetual': Not typical of its family in many ways and possibly the result of a cross with a Damask Rose. It forms a rather straggly, 6ft bush and is possibly best planted in groups of about three together, eighteen inches apart, so that each gives the other some support. It is very thorny and has small, greyish-green foliage. It flowers first in June, which is the time of the main flush, and then it is seldom without bloom until October, though there is no second big display. The flowers are about 3in across, very double with quilled petals, and are white, flushed pink, which quite soon fades to white. Only slight fragrance despite its supposed Damask connections, but altogether a wonderful rose, which dates from 1838. If grown on its own, give it some support. Healthy but only moderately good in rain.

R. *webbiana*: From Central Asia and the Himalayas, this rose will flower at the end of April in a mild spring. It is a graceful, arching, 6ft by 6ft shrub, which is almost thornless. The grey-green leaves are fern-like in their delicacy and form an appropriate background for the masses of 1½–2in single, pale pink blooms which are carried on the terminals of the shoots in clusters of five or six and have a sweet fragrance. Small, scarlet, bottle-shaped heps follow. AM 1955.

CHAPTER 6

The Gallica Roses

ALSO known as the Rose of Provins, these are the oldest of the old garden roses and appear in the ancestry of most of the others. They have almost thornless stems, some completely so, but many do bear prickles and bristles that will rub off at the touch of a finger. The leaves are rough to the touch, dark or medium green and often point upwards. The flower buds are round and blunt and the flowers are held aloft above the plants on firm stalks. They never nod as many of the old roses do. Their colour range includes pinks, mauves, purples and maroons, the intensity of which can vary quite a lot in different soils and situations. Striped sports are quite common and are some of the gayest of the old roses.

Gallicas form compact bushes, prone to sucker, and not usually more than 3–4ft high, so that they are ideal where space is limited. They thrive with the minimum of attention and on most soils and make some of the best roses for low hedges for garden division or lining paths or drives. No real pruning is needed as they constantly send up new growth from the base without its help, but removal in July, after flowering, of the old shoots which have died off will keep the centre of the bushes open. They will stand gentle clipping in winter if used for hedges.

Gallicas can get black spot, though I have never seen it affect them badly. Mildew is another matter and one or two are particularly prone, especially if the soil is very rich. So keep a lookout for it. They are all very hardy.

Alain Blanchard: Sometime earlier than 1825. This forms a 5ft by 3ft lax, arching bush with mid-green, rather unattractive foliage. It is an exception in the Gallica range in that it is very thorny, which indicates a cross at some time with another rose. The medium-sized, rather cupped, almost single flowers have golden stamens surrounded by crimson-scarlet petals, soon becoming mottled with maroon. The heps are pear-shaped. A more attractive rose than my description has, I think, made it sound. Taking it detail by detail does not really convey the over-all effect.

Belle de Crécy: Nearly thornless, lax, arching branches covered in matt, leaden-green leaves, bear flowers in June which are some of the most beautiful of all. They are very fragrant and open a rich, purplish pink, which quickly changes to wonderful blends of lilac, purple, slate grey and soft wild rose. The profusion of bloom has to be seen to be believed, though it should not have a dry and hot summer to give of its best. I have seen it said that a late frost will distort some of the flowers, but I have never experienced this myself. Not being a very erect grower, it will probably benefit from some support from surrounding shrubs.

Camaieux: 1830. Not a very strong grower, only reaching about 4ft by 2ft and one of the few Gallicas really needing good soil. The flowers are, however, sensational. The opening bloom is soft pink, striped and splashed with carmine-purple, the colours

1		2
3	4	5
6	7	8

merging after the first day, though in hot sunny weather the stripes fade to purple or grey with a white background before they do so. Finally the loosely arranged petals become a soft, uniform, lilac grey, but whatever the colour blending, and you can have all the stages on the bush at one time (late June), it is very beautiful. The heps are an anticlimax in this case. Rich fragrance.

Cardinal de Richelieu: 1840. An upright, compact bush with smooth leaves for a change and sumptuous, 3in, very double flowers of a dusky maroon-purple which reflex their petals on opening and reveal a white eye. With age they can become a bit untidy and fade to a dusty purple. They come in small clusters. The early colouring is very rich but do not expect the glowing red of a cardinal's robe. Shiny, dark green wood and few thorns. As this is a hybrid with quite a lot of the influence of a non-Gallica parent, it is one that is not at its best on poor, dry soils and needs good cultivation.

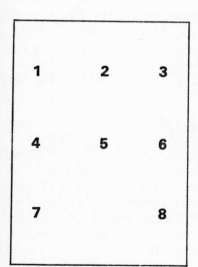

1	2	3
4	5	6
7		8

PLATE 12

Bourbon and Hybrid Perpetual roses

Charles de Mills: A low, wide bush, about 4ft by 4ft, flowering in June and July, growing vigorously and very free-blooming, this one has flowers that are unique. I have seen the opening buds described as looking like small, sliced-off beetroot, which fits them very well but gives no hint of the beauties to come. The flowers open into great multi-petalled, cup-shaped blooms which hold their form well for a long time. The colours are the most pleasing blends of plum-crimson, purple and maroon and of the greatest richness. Not to be missed. The weight of the blooms is such that they can do with some support.

Empress Josephine: Also called R. *francofurtana* and known since before 1583. It is a 4ft by 3ft bush which begins to flower in mid to late June and is well-branched, tough and reliable. The flowers are not as strongly scented as the others in this group, but otherwise just as good. They are large and moderately full and of a clear, purplish-rose, veined and shaded rosy pink. They are rather loosely formed, with waved petals, and are followed by large heps.

Jenny Duval: A 4ft by 3ft bush, flowering in June. The very full blooms open from long, coiled buds (not typical of the Gallicas) and are of a deep cherry-crimson shading to violet-grey in the centre. When fully opened the bases of the petals can be seen to be a creamy yellow, blending in with the yellow anthers. The flowers last well and are fragrant.

Officinalis: Also known as The Apothecary's Rose as it was used in times past for medicinal purposes and, as The Red Rose of Lancaster, this is a very ancient rose indeed. It forms a low, spreading bush, about 4ft by 4ft, well branched and with good foliage standing well out from the shoots in the typical Gallica manner, and with showy heps in the autumn. If on its own roots it suckers very freely. The 2½in flowers are semi-double and of a fiery crimson with pale yellow stamens, fading to purple-crimson. This is the rose that gave the name, The Provins Rose, to the Gallicas as it was in the town of Provins, not far from Paris, that it was first grown for its medicinal properties.

Rosa Mundi: Also known as R. *gallica versicolor*, this is another rose of great antiquity, a sport from Officinalis to which the odd branch occasionally reverts, and first recorded in 1581. It is said to be named after Fair Rosamund, the mistress of Henry II, but as his dates are 1154–89, there is some doubt that it is really quite as old as that. Being sentimental, I believe implicitly that it is, and only with great reluctance reveal that there is uncertainty. At any rate, whatever its age, it is one of the most enchanting and showy of the old roses. June flowering over a long period, it has flowers of deep pink, splashed and striped with white, or the other way round if you prefer it. They are loosely formed and open flat, but with the petals attractively waved. The bush is compact and upright, about 4ft by 4ft, and makes an excellent low hedging plant, though it will, regrettably, almost certainly have to be sprayed for mildew.

Surpasse Tout: Not, despite its name, the best of the Gallicas, but certainly a good one, and the 3in double flowers are the nearest one can get to scarlet amongst the old roses. Actually they are a brilliant cerise-pink, veined a darker shade, fading a little with age, and with the many petals reflexing and infolded in the centre to a button eye. It is a bushy and sturdy grower to about 4–5ft and as much across.

Tricolore de Flandre: 1846. A small, 3ft by 3ft bush, flowering in June, with its large, very double flowers of creamy white, splashed and striped with soft purple, and with a fine veining of carmine on the cream. The petals are small and multitudinous, the outer ones folding backwards as the flower opens so that the blooms become pompons of great beauty.

Tuscany Superb: First recorded in 1848, this forms a typical, upright, bushy Gallica shrub, about 4 ft by 2 ft in width. The double flowers open flat and are of a blackish crimson with sometimes a white streak or two, and just a glimpse of the yellow stamens. It is not as sweet-smelling as most of the roses of this group, but makes up for this in out-suckering most of them if grown on its own roots. It may be lightly clipped over in early spring if it is used for a hedge, for which it is very suitable.

CHAPTER 7

The Damask Roses

THE Damask Roses, which are thought to have been brought to Britain in about 1524, are of very mixed parentage and are a very mixed family as a result. There are certain points in common and all have downy greyish foliage, strong, hooked thorns, and in many cases they have weak flower stalks so that the blooms tend to nod. The heps are usually narrow and longer than the very rounded ones of the Gallicas. Summer blooming only, except for the Autumn Damask, the flowers are frequently borne in clusters. They need good soil and the twiggy growths removed after flowering to encourage new flowering shoots to form for the following year. Strong shoots should be shortened as need be by about one-third in winter to ensure bushy, shapely plants. The flowers are either pink or white, with a wonderful perfume. Cuttings taken in late summer and autumn root very easily. All are very hardy.

Celsiana and St Nicholas are both small enough for the smallest garden. Quatre Saisons and York and Lancaster are really only worth their place in a large one, where they can be grown at least in part for their historical interest, rather than for great spectacle of bloom, though neither are unattractive.

The very name Damask conjures up visions of rich crimson colourings, but most true Damask roses are in light shades. Another illusion shattered, I am afraid.

Blush Damask: A 5ft by 6ft shrub which flowers in great profusion in about the middle of June, but the flowering period can be short. While they are there, however, they are some of the most striking, fully double and quartered, nodding, and reflexing into a ball of deep lilac-pink, paler at the edges of the petals. A very twiggy bush with dark green leaves.

Celsiana: Large, 4in, loosely-formed semi-double flowers in great profusion, the petals having a transparent texture and being of a lovely rose pink, deeper in the bud, with a strong fragrance and yellow anthers. It makes a vigorous 5ft by 4ft bush, flowering in June, and with smooth, greyish leaves. It dates from before 1750.

Madame Hardy: 1832. Many think that this has the most beautiful blooms of all the old roses. They open from buds with long calices and are sometimes slightly blush tinted at first. Fully expanded, they are of the purest white, quartered and with a green carpel in the centre. They come on the side shoots which are often long and may be weighed down by the weight of the clusters of flowers. June flowering over a long period, but the blooms are not too good in the rain. It grows to about 5–6ft and is supposed to spread out to about the same distance, but I have found it much more upright and, despite selected pruning to outside shoots, very tall and not more than 3ft across after about eight years. Matt, light to mid-green leaves which may mildew. Sweet scent.

Quatre Saisons: Also known as the Autumn Damask and certainly pre-Roman and probably grown at Pompeii. Not a very large bush, about 4ft by 3ft, with light green leaves. The double pink flowers can be quite showy but are of poor form, continuing, though not prolifically after the June flush, until October. Of great historic interest, however.

St Nicholas: 1950. A sturdy, free-flowering (in June and July), recent discovery among the Damasks. The 5in, semi-double, cupped flowers are of Dog Rose pink with golden stamens and red heps to follow. About 4ft high and spreading out to 4ft as well, it may need a little attention from the secateurs in spring to keep it shapely.

York and Lancaster: Sixteenth century. Also known as R. *damascena versicolor* and not to be confused with Rosa Mundi, which it often is, the latter being R. *gallica versicolor*, but both being pink and white. York and Lancaster has not the same freedom of flower, though it is a reasonably good performer in a hot summer, and its loosely double blooms are not often striped. They are, rather, particoloured, some blooms being pink, some white, and some with both pink and white petals. On good soils it will form a big, vigorous shrub of 6ft by 6ft, but for its flowers alone it is not worth growing except where there is plenty of space.

CHAPTER 8

The Alba Roses

ALTHOUGH the White Rose has a botanical name, it is not a species, being a cross between a Damask Rose and the Dog Rose, from which it gets its habit of growth and type of thorns and heps. This is a vigorous race and all but two on my list can go well over 6ft and as much across. Even Felicité Parmentier wants watching on a good soil, which really suits the Albas best. They are not very prone to sucker but will spread slowly if they are on their own roots. The strong stems tend to branch freely, gradually building up the bush over the years, and some will need drastic pruning now and again to keep the base of the bush well furnished, as they say in the trade. In addition an even more superb display of flowers than usual will be obtained by cutting back all the twiggy growth after flowering and the longer shoots by about one third in February, which will give the new flowering shoots for the following year a real boost. You may need stilts to reach them, however.

The flowers come in corymbs, have a sweet scent and, despite the name of the group, are pink as well as white.

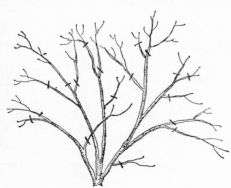

bud

Correct pruning cut

Cutting back the twig growth of a bush rose

Albas can easily be recognised, even out of flower, by the distinctive, bluish, grey-green, rather drooping leaves, which are usually disease-free. They are said to make good standards, though I have never seen them grown in this way and you would probably have to bud your own. Once flowering, in June and July, they are also supposed to do particularly well in the north of England. I have seen them performing well there, though once again I have no personal experience of Northern gardening.

R. *alba maxima*: Also known as the Great Double White and as the Jacobite Rose of Bonnie Prince Charlie, it forms a huge 7ft by 8ft shrub with the typical, drooping, leaden-green leaves of the family. The arching shoots bear in June and July a huge crop of flat, creamy white flowers with blush tints in the folds of the petals. They are fragrant and followed by oval heps. It will do well on a north wall, which makes it particularly useful – if you have a north wall for it to grow against.

R. *alba semi-plena*: Dating certainly from before 1600, this is

PLATE 13

Bourbon and Hybrid Perpetual roses

1		2
3	4	5
6	7	8

thought to be The White Rose of York, and was much used for the distillation of attar of roses in eastern Europe in times gone by. Generally similar to *alba maxima* (thought it may grow even bigger) except that the sprays of flowers are smaller and only semi-double, white and with golden stamens. Showy heps follow them.

Belle Amour: Salmon-pink, semi-double, cupped blooms with golden stamens, growing in clusters on a vigorous upright bush of about 6ft by 4ft, and appearing in mid- to late June with heps to follow. Slight, spicy scent and typical Alba leaves.

Celestial: Also known as Céleste, in the right place this will go up to 6ft and spread out to 7ft. The half-open buds are of exceptional beauty and open to almost transparent, soft pink, shell-like, semi-double 4in flowers, which look wonderful against the blue-grey leaves. They come in clusters of two or three and have a rich scent. Mid- to late June. One of the best, resulting in an AM in 1948.

1		2
3	4	5
6	7	8

Félicité Parmentier: 1836. A smaller bush, not usually over 4ft tall by about 3ft, though I have seen specimens considerably bigger. The creamy buds open in June to very double pompon flowers of the palest pink with still a hint of the original cream. It forms a bushy plant but is inclined to be more spreading and less upright than the other Albas.

Great Maiden's Blush: Very old, from prior to the fifteenth century, this rose was originally known in France as *Cuisse de Nymphe Emue* or Thigh of the Passionate Nymph. Why, oh why, was it changed? But it was, and I suppose Great Maiden's Blush is not a bad way to describe the clusters of very double mother-of-pearl blooms, though they tend to fade almost to white in time. It will grow to 6ft or more by about 5ft, and is the last of the Albas to come into bloom, waiting till fairly late in June, but carrying on well into July. Sweet scent. There is a smaller Maiden's Blush, which explains the Great in this one, which otherwise would make it sound like a six-foot hockey player who has just missed a sitter of a goal.

Koenigin von Danemarck: Often appearing in nursery lists under its translation, Queen of Denmark, this one dates from 1826 and is probably the best Alba for small gardens, growing on average to about 5ft by 4ft. Quite apart from its size, it is one of the loveliest of all the Albas for any garden, the carmine-pink buds opening and gradually reflexing to very double, quartered blooms of a soft rose pink with a button eye. They have a sweet scent.

It is of rather open, spindly growth for this family, but has the typical blue-grey leaves. Blooms in June and July and, like *alba maxima* can be used against a north wall.

Madame Plantier: There is some doubt as to whether this is a true Alba, but it is usually classed as such and I am not arguing the point. If well tended and on good soil, this is one that will go up a low tree or tall bush to 12ft or so, or it will make a dense, arching bush of about 6ft high and 6ft across. The leaves are a give-away as they are small and light green, not like the Albas at all. The blooms come in mid- to late June in large clusters, each a smallish pompon, creamy-white and fading to pure white, and with a green carpel in the centre of each. If suitably trained it will make a good 4–5ft hedge.

Maiden's Blush: This is the smaller of the two Maiden's Blush roses referred to above, which is generally similar to its bigger sister, though only growing to 5ft or so. The 2½in blush flowers open quite flat and I would say that they are not, perhaps, quite so double as in the other rose. Featured often in old paintings.

CHAPTER 9

The Centifolia Roses

ALSO known as Provence Roses just to make things more confusing when the Gallicas are known as Provins roses, these are
mainly rather open, lax, not to say ungainly growers, the very
thorny stems needing some support, either artificial or by close
planting. Petite de Hollande, De Meaux and Fantin-Latour are
perhaps the most compact, the first two being the smallest as well.

New shoots five feet long on the bigger ones are not uncom-
mon and should be shortened by one-third or even one-half in
February or the weight of the blooms near the ends may bow
them right down to the ground. Otherwise the same pruning
treatment as for the Albas may be carried out. The huge, drooping
leaves have five leaflets, each one about two inches long, and as
the rather weak-necked flowers also hang their heads on the long
arching canes, this is a real bloodhound of a rose. The flowers
themselves are, however, marvellous, and are of the kind which
most people think of when talking about old garden roses. In
other words this is the Cabbage Rose, but the formation of the
petals is actually much less like a cabbage than it is in many of the
Hybrid perpetuals and early Hybrid Teas. The outer petals are
large and enfold the closely-packed but much shorter centre ones,
so that you can peer right into the middle of the flower which,
being protected from strong sunshine, retains its depth of
colouring. They are richly scented.

Centifolias need good cultivation and are not proof against
mildew.

R. centifolia: The original Cabbage Rose, Rose of a Hundred
Leaves or *Rose des Peintres*. My general description of the group

fits this one exactly. The huge, globular, scented blooms are of a
soft pink and grow on a bush about 5ft tall, spreading out to 4ft.

Chapeau de Napoleon: Also known as the Crested Moss though it is not really a true Moss Rose as the mossing only occurs on the edges and tips of the calyx. Its rich, rose-pink flowers, not quite as globular as the typical Centifolia, come in June and July on a bush about 5ft by 4ft, which is perhaps rather more slender and graceful than the type. 1827.

De Meaux: 1814. Not at all a conventional Centifolia, as it forms a much more erect, though still arching, bush only about 3ft 6in in height and with small, light green foliage. The light pink flowers are small, only about 1in across, and go through the pompon stage until they finally open flat. Sweetly scented, they appear in early June and the bush will bloom even more freely if it is reasonably hard pruned and thinned out every year. It tends to much branched and twiggy growth.

Fantin-Latour: 3½in, cup-shaped, pale pink flowers, opening flat with a button eye, very double and growing in clusters of between two and five. June/July flowering, the bush is a sturdy grower with dark, smooth leaves and should reach 6ft and as much if not more across. AM 1959. AGM 1968.

Petite de Hollande: This has typical soft pink Centifolia flowers, cupped and with masses of short petals in the centre and with the colour also deeper there, though they are on the small side in keeping with the bush itself. It grows only to about 3ft or a little more, the arching canes spreading out to about the same distance. June/July.

Robert le Diable: An untidy grower due to its rather weak branches. They will reach 4ft but badly need something to lean on to keep the flowers off the ground. The blooms show that a Gallica Rose is somewhere in the background as they are not globular and the outer petals quickly reflex. They are a rich purple with slate-blue and violet shadings, with the odd centre petal sometimes a vivid cerise or scarlet in startling contrast. A beautiful rose and worth the extra trouble it needs.

Tour de Malakoff: one of the really big ones with heavy, arching branches going up to 6ft and needing a tough prop or perhaps to be grown as a pillar rose. It also needs good soil to give of its best, but again the extra effort is more than worth while. It has huge, 5in, loosely double blooms of a vivid carmine with lilac edging to the petals when newly open, the carmine changing gradually through violet to a bluish, dusky grey before the petals fall. A quite breath-taking transformation. 1856.

CHAPTER 10

The Moss Roses

THE Moss Roses are sports from the Centifolias and they are alike in many ways, though they tend to be rather more robust growers and more erect in habit. They were introduced into this country by Dutch growers about 200 years ago.

The really distinctive thing about the Moss Roses is, of course, the moss. This consists of green, reddish or even brown glandular projections all over the flower stalks and sepals, which are sticky and fragrant and which must have come originally, I suppose, from some mutation like the Green Rose. It does not sound particularly attractive described in this way, and frankly I would like the roses just as well if they had not got it. But they have, and it does give them a certain old-world charm, perhaps simply because of the period cottage garden-poke bonnet-crinoline associations. It was a white Moss Rose that Sergeant Cuff was arguing about with the gardener in Wilkie Collins's *The Moonstone*.

The colour range covers the pinks, crimson and maroon-purple of the old roses, though there is one modern yellow called Golden Moss. They are very liable to sport, like good cultivation, and should have some of the old shoots cut right back every year as the best blooms come on the growths of the previous summer. Growing them as standards is unusual but effective and they can be rooted readily from cuttings taken in late autumn, though the plants will not be as vigorous as budded ones.

For small gardens almost any of the Moss Rose are suitable, even the huge William Lobb if it is grown as a climber. Mousseline, with lovely, cupped pink blooms, is one of the most compact, has a good flush of flowers in June, and then blooms intermittently until October unlike the others which are once-flowering. Mildew is a possibility.

Capitaine John Ingram: Introduced in 1856, this is a rather late-flowering and quite bushy shrub, which will reach 5ft by 4ft. It has dark green leaves and small, full-petalled, rosette-type flowers of a vinous purple with a lighter reverse. Apart from the button eye, they look like small, velvety peonies, fragrant and with dark red moss on the buds and sepals.

Duchesse de Verneuil: Fair-sized flowers, not as big as some but making up for it in showiness, for they are of a strong pink, lighter on the reverse and with a button eye. A 5ft bush, spreading out well. June/July.

Général Kleber: Very similar to the Duchess above and introduced at the same time, in 1856, but the Général has bigger flowers, up to 5in across. They are of mother-of-pearl pink with a silky sheen, opening flat with a button eye. Bright green leaves and moss. Rich fragrance.

Gloire de Mousseux: 1856 seems to have been a vintage year, for it also produced this one, a robust plant of about 4ft by 4ft with

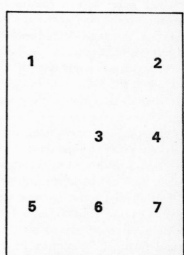

plentiful light green leaves and light green moss which sometimes runs quite a long way down the stem. Richly scented, the
flowers are probably the biggest of all, a clear pink with infolded
centres and button eyes. The colour fades to a pale blush with
age.

Henri Martin: Late June and July flowering, this has clusters of
medium-sized double flowers in light crimson. It forms a very
thorny bush about 5ft by 4ft with plenty of fresh green leaves
but rather scanty moss. 1863.

Mousseline: An individualist among the Moss Roses, in that the
flowers, after the first flush in June, appear continuously right
through until October. They are medium to large, double and
cup-shaped, of a soft flesh-pink and sweetly fragrant. The buds
and flower stalks have short, brownish-green moss. The bush
is compact and not over tall, rarely topping 4ft and spreading
out to about the same measure. Also known as Alfred de Dalmas.
1855.

1	**2**	**3**
4		**5**
6	**7**	**8**

PLATE 16

Hybrid Musk roses   *page*

1. Buff Beauty   117
2. Cornelia   117
3. Danae   117
4. Felicia   117
5. Francesca   117
6. Hamburg   117
7. Magenta   118
8. Moonlight   118

Nuits de Young: 1851. The darkest of all the Moss Roses, having neat, dark green leaves with coppery overtones and blooms which form symmetrical rosettes, singly and in clusters, of a velvety maroon, which fades a little as the blooms age. Yellow stamens light them up but the moss is a dark, brownish-red, sometimes touched with purple. Strong fragrance. An erect, wiry, bush, slender for a Moss, about 4ft by 3ft. It looks wonderful with silver-leaved plants.

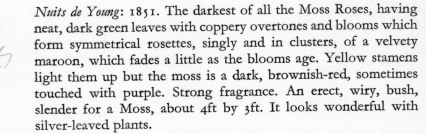

William Lobb: 1855. This Moss will go up to 6ft or more if it is used as a short climber, which is the best way to use it if space is restricted. In a border it will spread out as tall as it is high, but it is not an elegant grower. The blooms make up for this by being of great beauty, growing on long, very thorny stems in large clusters. They are very double, about 3in across and of a dark fuchsia purple with a light magenta reverse, paling in time to a soft lilac-grey. The buds and flower stalks are very heavily mossed.

CHAPTER 11

The China and Portland Roses

MOST of the China Roses are short, rather spindly shrubs which do well in mixed flower borders. They come into flower early, generally at the beginning of June, and it was, you may remember, their habit of carrying on flowering until the autumn that made them such an asset to early rose breeders and led to the perpetual flowering rose of today. They are not notable for their scent, but make up for it with their profusion of bloom, provided they have a warm, sunny position. Prune to about three buds the first spring after planting and from then on remove short, twiggy and old spent wood in February each year. They will be quite happy on poorish soil, but will, like all the others, repay good cultivation.

Bloomfield Abundance: 1920. Said to have been described as Bloomfield Ambulance in someone's catalogue, this is a large shrub (the first one would be, when I have said that most of them are small) with tiny, thimble-sized, flesh-pink blooms which resemble Hybrid Teas in the bud but open into rather formless rosettes. Despite its size, the bush is quite open and airy, nearly thornless and with small, rather pointed leaves. It bears smallish sprays of bloom in early June and later sends up very vigorous shoots four feet or more in length with enormous corymbs of flowers at the ends and further smaller sprays from the side shoots. This rose is often confused with and sometimes sold as Cécile Brunner (see below). It is very alike in many ways, but it grows much larger – about 6ft by 7ft, or more if the conditions are absolutely right for it – and the flowers, which are otherwise identical, have very long, leafy lobes to the calyx. The buds appear to be wearing a plume and this is not present in Cécile Brunner. AM 1953.

Cécile Brunner: Very much like the above, except in size, only reaching about 4ft by 3ft, with open, not particularly robust growth, which will take two to three years to reach full stature. Can be used successfully for bedding where charm is more important than a jazzy show. Do not overdo the p uning, only removing weak growth, and with good soil it will reward you with a non-stop succession of button-hole blooms. 1881. Light scent and good weather resistance.

Little White Pet: 1879. There seems to be some doubt whether or not this really is a China Rose, some holding that it is a sport from the rambler Félicité et Perpétue. Toss for it if you like, but I am not responsible for putting it among the Chinas, with which it is usually classed. But whatever its history it will give you a non-stop show of bloom from early June onwards on a very small, 2ft by 2ft bush, ideal for the rockery or for small groupings at the front of a shrub border, provided it gets full sun. The 1½in flowers come in large and small clusters, are creamy-white to blush, and open flat and extremely double. The small, matt, dark green foliage makes a pleasing contrast. Do not overdo the pruning. Light scent.

Natalie Nypels: 1919. Another charming little rose, useful for bedding on a small scale, for it only grows to about 2ft by 2ft, though it is bushy and well filled out with dark green leaves. From early June onwards it will be covered with large clusters of 2½in semi-double, cupped, rose-pink flowers which fade whit e and are sweetly scented. It is as good as, if not better than, most of the floribundas of similar size. There are not many of this colouring and none at all as strongly perfumed. It can mildew.

Perle d'Or: A sturdy bush, a good deal bigger than the last three, reaching 4ft by 3ft, but not unlike a rather larger version of Cécile Brunner in many ways. The flowers, however, open from yellow buds and when fully blown are cream, shading to apricot in the centre. 1883.

Serratipetala: To most people the shrub roses that have their petals fringed like a pink or Sweet William are F. J. Grootendorst and its pink sport, Pink Grootendorst. They are certainly the best known and the easiest to get hold of, but for a change (assuming you have something to change from) why not try pursuing this one. It dates from some time prior to 1912 and makes a smaller bush than the Grootendorsts, growing only to about 5ft by 5ft, which can be useful on occasions. It is open-growing with rather sparse leaves. The flowers are crimson with a lighter centre, the colour intensifying in hot weather but becoming paler in the autumn.

Slater's Crimson China: Also known as R. *semperflorens*, this one goes back to 1792 and is the original dark crimson China Rose from which all dark red roses are descended. Probably not one to pick if you are only choosing a few shrub roses, for it is not very robust except in a warm, sheltered spot, when it can make quite a show. It needs generous treatment of the soil and should not be pruned hard. Old and twiggy growth may be removed in February or March and new shoots shortened by not more than a third. Good scent. 4ft by 3ft.

R. *viridiflora*: Other names are The Green Rose and, less kindly, R. *monstrosa*, which shows the opinion some people must have had of it. Actually I rather like it, though it is certainly an oddity. It dates from 1855 and makes a light, open bush about 4ft by 3ft which with me is longer in flower than any other rose. It starts usually in April and as I write this, in January, it is still going strong, despite several frosty nights. It is growing, too, quite happily in the shade of a mountain ash, but having said all that, it must be admitted that it is not a rose that makes its presence felt. You could easily miss it if you did not know it was there, for the small flowers merge in with the rather pointed green leaves. They come in clusters from blue-green buds which have long calices and which look like ordinary rose buds. However, they open with rather confused leafy green "petals" which take on brown and purple streaks, which are unusual to say the least of it. St Peter greets every flower arranger with a bunch of these at the gates of Heaven.

THE PORTLAND ROSES

There is no real reason for including these in the chapter mainly devoted to the China Roses, except that there are not enough of them generally available to form a chapter on their own and they do have a link with the Chinas, which were one of their parents. They, in turn, helped to produce the Hybrid Perpetuals, so they are an important if small group. Cut away spent and twiggy wood in spring.

Comte de Chambord: Probably the best of the Portlands, this forms a 4ft by 3ft reasonably vigorous bush, which starts to flower in mid-June and is seldom without some blooms from then until the frosts. They are very double, opening to rather muddled quartering, and are extremely fragrant. The colour is bright pink, paler at the edges of the petals. It dates from about 1860.

Jacques Cartier: 1868. A shrub with the light green, rather pointed leaves of the group, upright and erect to 4ft by 3ft. The flowers are large, very double and quartered, and of a strong pink, paling almost to white at the edges of the petals. As the flower ages the pink fades and the whole bloom becomes rather shapeless, which probably makes it not as good a bet as Comte de Chambord, though it is very lovely early on and is, of course, recurrent, starting into flower in mid-June.

CHAPTER 12

The Bourbon and Hybrid Perpetual Roses

THE Bourbon Roses had a good run for their money and were probably more popular for a period of something like fifty years than any rose before the coming of the Hybrid Tea and floribunda. Their colours blend well with the older varieties and many of their flowers have a similar form, together with the silky petals of the China Roses. There is a June/July flush and then another in September, which in some varieties is much the better of the two as the early flowers can be malformed. The blooms come on the current year's growth as well as on that from previous years, in which the Bourbons differ from the older roses.

There is considerable variety in habit of growth, but a typical Bourbon would be 5 or 6ft tall and about 3 to 4ft across, well branched but generally upright. Many are on the large side if space is limited, but three of the best, La Reine Victoria and its sport Mme Pierre Oger, and Louise Odier, though fairly tall, do not spread out too much. There are few gardens that could not accommodate at least one of them and they should be in all. Souvenir de la Malmaison can also be kept within bounds, but it is really only one for a historical collection as the flowers cannot be guaranteed to open well in a damp summer. This is my own experience of it, though I know of one grower at least (his soil is chalky), who strongly disagrees. His Bourbons and HPs also do marvellously without any pruning at all, but lack of space in a small garden may make this necessary. I find it gives better results myself and if you do decide to do it, this is the way.

Prune short, twiggy growth after blooming to encourage new flowering shoots, and in December spur back side shoots to about three eyes and reduce the main shoots by about one third. Actually, of course, you should do the two operations the other way round, or you will be spurring back side shoots which you will subsequently be removing with the main ones. As near as a touch I landed you with more work than is necessary, but however you prune, the more vigorous Bourbons will romp away and the tallest will almost certainly need some support, and pretty substantial support at that. The best flowers are produced on the shoots which develop after the first flowering, which explains why the autumn crop is usually of higher quality.

The early Hybrid Teas and the later Hybrid Perpetuals looked very much alike, the former of course being developed from the latter. La France, usually now considered the first Hybrid Tea and produced in 1867, was first classified as a Hybrid Perpetual, but the Hybrid Perpetuals one can get from nurseries today are generally fairly distinct from the modern, high-centred Hybrid Teas. They were called Hybrid Perpetuals because they were considered to be perpetual flowering, which by the standards of their time they probably were. In fact the majority flower profusely in mid- to late June, a little later than most Hybrid Teas, carrying over well into July. There is then a longish gap until the second crop of bloom in September/October.

This second crop can be very disappointing, though it seems to vary enormously, which leads to conflicting opinions about certain roses. To take one instance, I have seen Prince Camille de Rohan described as a free bloomer in the autumn – and not in a grower's catalogue, either – but this is not my experience of it. All I can do is describe each one as I myself have found it, only adding that, because of their mixed ancestry, certain Hybrid Perpetuals do not even try to flower twice. Everyone is agreed about these ones.

None of them are at their best in continuous hot weather, but thrive in the usual mixture we have in this country. That was one of the reasons they were so popular here in their heyday, but never received the same acclaim in, for instance, the USA.

Probably in a small garden only one or two Hybrid Perpetuals would be enough for, if not heavily pruned, they can make big bushes five feet or more in height and a good yard across. As such, they can be fine specimen shrubs or can be planted in a group of three or so, either one of a kind or mixed. The flowers are generally large, either cupped or globular, and in many cases in one, unshaded, distinct colour, covering a range from white, through pink, to crimson. Two exceptions to the usual flower forms are Reine des Violettes, which has flat, quartered blooms much more like a Gallica rose, and Roger Lambelin, whose crimson, white-edged blooms have scalloped edges.

All can get mildew and black spot, and all thrive on a good loam and are not too frightened of a little shade. Prune to three or four buds the first spring after planting and otherwise follow the pattern described in Chapter 3.

Adam Messerich: Bourbon (B) 1920 and 6ft by 5ft. Its first flowers come in mid-June and there is a good second crop in September, but there are few if any in between. They are large, semi-double and rather loosely formed and of a warm pink which holds well. Vigorous growth as a shrub or for a pillar, with good foliage and a strong fragrance. Long stems for cutting.

Boule de Neige: (B) In flower from mid-June to October, this forms a rather slender, erect shrub to 5ft, with the small clusters of crimson buds opening to 2½in creamy-white blooms, the outer petals of which curve back and have a pink flush at their edges. There are also short stems bearing individual flowers, and in late summer shoots develop up to four or five feet long, which carry blooms along a foot or more of their length. Smooth, dark green leaves and a sweet scent. One of the loveliest. 1867.

Commandant Beaurepaire: (B) One of the most prolific June/July flowerers, but little if anything afterwards. The blooms are borne in large and small clusters on almost every shoot, are cupped but not quite fully double, and are of a deep pink, splashed and striped with maroon, purple and lighter pink, which makes a most striking display. They are sweetly scented. It makes a thorny bush some 6ft by 5ft with yellowish-green leaves, which will throw 6ft shoots in the autumn, seldom, unfortunately, crowned with more than the odd flower.

Ferdinand Pichard: 1921. A lonely orphan which no family seems to want as it is sometimes classed as a Bourbon and sometimes as a Hybrid Perpetual or a Hybrid Tea. It came from America in 1921 and did not, apparently, bring its birth certificate with it, though there is certainly quality in its breeding and it is one of the few really perpetual striped roses. It forms a 4ft by 4ft, rather spreading shrub with medium-sized cupped flowers in small clusters, which are striped crimson and pink on a white ground. There are generally some on the bush at all times from June onwards and they are well set off by the matt yellowish-green leaves which are not, unfortunately, proof against mildew. My two made a slow start, but this was because I landed squarely with one foot in the middle of each of them when slipping from a ladder when I was cutting a hedge in their first August. They must have thought they were back in the orphanage, but have borne no resentment since. Call it a Fitz-Bourbon.

Frau Karl Druschki: Hybrid Perpetual (HP) or HT – no one seems to be sure, but there is more reason in this case as it dates from the time when Hybrid Teas were still being developed from Hybrid Perpetuals and it was often difficult to distinguish one from the other. It does not, however, have the continuity of bloom one would expect from a Hybrid Tea, flowering first in June and July and then resting until September. It is also occasionally known as Snow Queen because of its flowers of the purest white. They are sometimes streaked with pink in the bud, but there is no sign of this once the bloom opens, and there is no trace of scent, either. The flowers tend to come in clusters, especially in the autumn and, as the buds are very close together and the open blooms large I find it best to do some disbudding so that they can develop their full beauty. If they are kept only one to a stem they will be very large indeed and, despite the fact that it dates from 1901, many people think that it is still the best white rose of the Hybrid Tea type. Until the coming of the Hybrid Tea Pascali I would have agreed with them. The latter has smaller flowers, certainly, but it is very nearly rain-proof and is not prone to mildew and you cannot say the same about Frau Karl Druschki on either count. Frau Karl is a vigorous grower up to 5 or 6ft, rather upright, and will send up very long canes which are best pegged down. Light green, matt foliage. AM 1902.

Général Jacqueminot: (HP) Raised by a French amateur in 1853, this one has the most wonderful scarlet-crimson double flowers and is one of the forebears of Crimson Glory and Ena Harkness. There are, in fact, well over five hundred roses descended from it and it was so popular at one time that it acquired a nickname, General Jack – or it may simply have been that no one could pronounce its second name. It also has the distinction of being one of the first Hybrid Perpetuals to have long enough petals to form a globular bloom, rather than the multitudes of short petals in the older varieties. It retained their wonderful perfume, however. The 4ft by 3ft bush gives a bold display in mid-June and July but is not quite so free in the autumn, when it can also get a little mildew. Better than many in hot weather.

George Arends: (HP) 1910. Coming into flower in mid- to late June, George Arends has the scrolled bud of the Hybrid Tea, which develops into a flower of the most lovely transparent rose-pink with a touch of cream in the reverse of the petals. A 6ft by 3ft upright grower with light green leaves which can mildew in the autumn. Sweet scent.

George Dickson: (HP) A very strong grower up to 5ft and suitable for pegging down. It has very large cupped blooms of deep crimson-purple with a wonderful scent. The flower stalks tend to be weak, so that the flowers nod. Unfortunately a bad one for mildew, but a magnificent rose none the less.

Honorine de Brabant: (B) A rampant grower that will certainly need some support, perhaps from one of the triangular structures I described in Chapter 3. It will reach 6ft by 6ft, thick and bushy, with large, light green foliage and rather loosely formed, not quite fully double, cupped and quartered blooms. These are of a pale, rosy mauve, spotted and striped a darker mauve and crimson and they are sweetly fragrant. The September blooming is good, better than Commandant Beaurepaire, of which this is otherwise a paler counterpart.

Hugh Dickson: (HP) 1905. Starts into bloom as a rule much earlier than most Hybrid Perpetuals, sometimes at the end of May in a warm spring. The flowers are fully double and of a rich crimson, shaded scarlet, very freely produced, the autumn crop coming on the young shoots formed during the summer. The early flowers, which tend to nod due to the weak flower stalks, grow mostly at the tips of the very long canes unless these are pegged down. As they can reach about 9ft (the canes, not the flowers), pegging or training on a pillar or other support is almost a must.

Kathleen Harrop: (B) 1919. This is a sport from the Bourbon short climber Zéphirine Drouhin (which see) and similar in many ways, though it is not quite so vigorous and the flowers are of a much lighter, clear pink with a cerise reverse. It will reach 7ft by 5ft, blooming well in June and July but, like its parent, with a sometimes disappointing second crop. Good scent and some mildew likely in the autumn.

La Reine Victoria: (B) This is one of the loveliest of the Bourbons, growing to about 5ft but remaining fairly upright. As it only spreads to about 3ft it can be accommodated in quite a small space, so that it is one of the best for a small garden. The blooms are quite exquisite, cupped in shape and with paper-thin, shell-like petals of the most delicate pink and sweet scent. They can stain in wet weather and the foot-stalks of the flowers are rather prone to mildew, which can spread to the leaves if not sprayed promptly. It is often recommended to be grouped with its sport Mme Pierre Oger and with Louise Odier, all of which are of similar type. In fact, until I looked at their dates of introduction, I always thought that Louise Odier was a sport of La Reine Victoria, and I am sure that I have seen it so described, though now I want to check this I cannot of course find any such reference. 1872.

Louise Odier: (B) Dating from 1851, this is perhaps a rather more vigorous grower than La Reine Victoria, reaching 6ft by 4ft, very upright and with the slender shoots apt to be weighed down with the weight of bloom unless they are tied in. It has the same perfect cupped flower formation, but the pink this time has more than a hint of lilac in it. It is a rose that can, I believe, be quite successfully pegged down, though I have never grown it in this way. Pretty continuous flowering after the first June flush and some mildew in the autumn unless watched.

Madame Ernst Calvat: (B) A sport from Mme Isaac Pereire (the next on the list) and a tremendous grower with attractive red-tinted young leaves. It forms a 7ft by 5ft shrub which will probably need some support and which will make a good pillar rose. The blooms are very large and double, globular, quartered and with crinkly petals of a silvery peach, deepening in the centre to deep rose pink and with a darker reverse. Wonderful scent and a good show of bloom in the autumn. 1888.

Madame Isaac Pereire: Enormously vigorous and with blooms of a size to match, though in the first flush in late June some of them can be malformed. In the autumn, however, they are truly magnificent, some of the most richly scented of all roses, cupped, very double and sometimes quartered, and of a deep carmine-pink with a slightly paler reverse. It is a colour which blends well with the old roses but needs keeping away from the bright modern oranges and reds. A 7 to 8ft by 6ft shrub on its own, it will benefit from the support of a pillar, or it can be grown as a short climber. My two I have grown from cuttings and after six years they are a good deal smaller than the parent plant from which they came – perhaps five feet by three, which would seem to be the way to have them if your space is limited. The flowers are every bit as big and sumptuous. Some mildew in the autumn is likely. 1880.

Madame Pierre Oger: (B) The third of the trio I mentioned when describing La Reine Victoria and dating from 1887. The same delicate cupped blooms in clusters of five or six and of a creamy blush which takes on a deep pink flush in hot sunshine, as is the habit with some of the China Roses. It forms once again a narrow, upright bush, 6ft by 3ft, with mid-green matt leaves which, together with the foot-stalks of the flowers will need watching for mildew. The rather slender shoots may droop under the weight of bloom and need tying in, more especially during the June flush when the flowers are larger than they are in the autumn. Fine scent.

Mrs John Laing: (HP) 1887. A stiff, upright-growing Hybrid Perpetual that has been a great favourite since its introduction over eighty years ago. The 4½in flowers are very full, globular in form, and of a bright, silvery rose-pink, with a hint of lilac. It is probably the most free-flowering of the Hybrid Perpetuals and very persistent, with an excellent autumn crop of bloom which seems to be impervious to rain. Not as tall as some, reaching only 5ft by 3ft on average, but it can be made into a fuller looking bush by tying the longer growths down to the base of the plant. Sweet scent and healthy, light green, rather small leaves.

Prince Camille de Rohan: (HP) 1861. A romantic name and a dramatic looking flower to bear out its promise. Only of medium size, the blooms are double, shapely and of a velvety blackish crimson, with hints of both maroon and purple. As a plant it is one of the less vigorous Hybrid Perpetuals, rarely exceeding 4ft in height, and after the June/July flush it is apt to be shy of repeating. More than most it needs a cool season to give of its best, but the blooms do not mind rain and are richly scented. Very liable to mildew and can be affected by rust. A parent of Roger Lambelin.

Reine des Violettes: (HP) As its name would suggest, the sumptuous double, quartered blooms are violet-purple when fully expanded, a strong earlier hint of cerise quickly vanishing. The greyish green leaves form a perfect foil for the flowers, and come on a big, 6ft, spreading bush if it is given good cultivation. Otherwise it can be rather short-lived and lacking in its true vigour. Fairly hard pruning in February is also needed to give the best results, but if well looked after this can be one of the most beautiful and also one of the most continuous flowering of all in its group. Except for its size, it resembles a Gallica rather than a Hybrid Perpetual.

Roger Lambelin: (HP) The flowers of this one are almost unique amongst roses, only medium sized and of a dark maroon-purple, but with the edges of the petals scalloped and bordered with a thin line of white. The other rose that has rather similar colourings and marking is Baron Girod de l'Ain, which is said to be more vigorous and better for growing on poor soils. I have never tried the latter, but I have not had any particular trouble with Roger Lambelin, which has to put up with a pretty stingy diet in my garden, though I do try to give it that little bit extra when the other roses are not looking. It is not, even at its best, a large or very vigorous grower, reaching about 4ft by 3ft, fairly open in habit and with light green matt leaves which are not immune to mildew and on which I have seen a little black spot. However, the flowers, which are sweetly scented, make up for a lot. 1890.

Souvenir de la Malmaison: (B) A lusty, bushy grower to about 5ft by 4ft, which really needs good, hot weather to give of its best. In a damp summer the flowers will not open well and can be most disappointing, though the second crop in September does not seem to be so badly affected. Under favourable conditions it seems to be almost always in flower, the large 5–6in blooms being very full, opening flat and quartered and being of the most delicate creamy blush pink, though again in the first crop some can be divided and malformed. Not a rose for a limited collection because of its unpredictability, but more than worth taking a chance on if you have a big garden. Fine for a pillar, when it will go up to 6ft. Healthy.

Ulrich Brunner: (HP) 1882. A very robust grower with shoots up to 6ft in length, which need to be pegged down unless the rose is used on a pillar. The medium-sized flowers are double, and loosely cupped on opening, and of a brilliant carmine-red which often fades quickly. Good foliage which does not seem to be so prone to mildew as others of the type. Sweet scent and reasonably good repeat in the autumn, though this seems to vary from year to year.

Variegata di Bologna: (B) 1909. The flowers on this 6ft by 5ft bush are very double, cupped in shape, with dark crimson-purple striping on a lilac-white ground and full quartering of the petals. Sometimes the odd petal or two in the centre of the flower is purple only, without the striping, and occasionally a flower or two will sport back to a crimson-purple parent. The first flush of bloom is memorable, but the repeat is not to be relied on and can be very disappointing. A good, lusty grower, bushy and with good foliage when young, but liable to black spot from about July onwards. Can be used successfully as a pillar rose and generally in need of support of some kind to keep it from looking untidy. Very fragrant.

Zigeuner Knabe: Also known as Gipsy Boy, this one dates from

1909 and forms an arching, spreading shrub, not typical at all of the Bourbons. The flowers come in clusters all along the branches, are about 3in in diameter, very double and open flat. In colour they are of a deep crimson-purple, white at the base of the petals and sometimes showing a glimpse of golden stamens. I have never been able to detect much scent and it is once-flowering only, though over a long period in June and July. It will reach 5ft in height, spreading out to considerably more than this, so that it is really best grown amongst other shrubs on which it can lean. The heps are quite attractive in the autumn, but not as spectacular as some. I have found that it does extremely well from cuttings taken in September, and that the resulting bushes are every bit as vigorous as ones budded on to brier stock, though I am not yet in a position to say how long-lived they may be in comparison. The many prickles give it a good hand-hold if it is allowed to scramble into other shrubs, which it loves to do.

CHAPTER 13

The Rugosa Roses

THESE are all descended from the wild Rugosa Rose of Japan and China and are probably the best of all roses for the attraction of their fresh green foliage, coupled with continuous bloom throughout the summer and autumn. Their leaves are very distinct, being deeply ribbed, which gives them a crinkled appearance found in no other roses. They will grow in almost any soil, make good seaside shrubs, and will even thrive amongst tree roots provided they are in full sun. Many of them make good hedges, clothed with leaves right down to the ground and quite impenetrable, for they are all incredibly prickly.

When used as hedges, they will stand a certain amount of clipping over in winter to keep them in shape, but otherwise they require little pruning except the tipping back of new growths and the occasional removal of an odd spent branch or two. The single forms have noteworthy heps, but to keep continuity of flowering, old flower heads should be removed, at least after the first flush of bloom in June and July. The Grootendorst types, being double, do not make heps and will continue to flower quite happily with no dead-heading at all.

The heps of the Rugosas are, incidentally, very rich in vitamin C and make good rose-hep syrup and jam. And in case your pheasants are looking peaky, Frank Cant's catalogue of 1964/5 tells us that "partridges and pheasants are very partial to the seeds and pulp of this fruit and belts of these roses should be planted in all game preserves." Mind their legs and tail feathers when you are pruning.

Rugosas are so tough and bushy that they are also used on the continent as traffic barriers between the lanes of motorways.

The colours of this group range from the purest white of Blanc Double de Coubert, through the pink of Frau Dagmar Hastrup, to the deep wine red of Roseraie de l'Hay, and there is one comparatively modern hybrid, Agnes, which is yellow. The form of the flowers varies enormously as Rugosas have been crossed with many other varieties whose characteristics they have taken on in some cases, though the typical Rugosa leaf is almost always retained.

For a small garden, Belle Pointevine, Frau Dagmar Hastrup, Fimbriata, and Pink Grootendorst should not be difficult to accommodate, though several of the others like Roseraie de l'Hay, Blanc Double de Coubert, Scabrosa and Schneezwerg can be contained within reasonable proportions by moderately hard pruning, which they do not resent. Max Graf, a hybrid with a rambler, grows prostrate along the ground and here again judicious pruning after flowering (it only flowers once, late in June) can restrict its wanderings.

Agnes: This came to us from Canada in 1922 and is the only yellow Rugosa, the result of a cross with R. *foetida persiana*. It flowers early in June but is not as recurrent as most of the other Rugosas and the blooms are rather short-lived. They are about 2in in diameter, forming fully double pompons of a pale amber-yellow, shading to cream at the edges of the petals and with a sweet scent. The bush is tall, probably up to 7ft, but its spreading, arching branches can look rather straggly. Very good bright green leaves.

R. *rugosa alba*: Makes a great spreading, leafy bush, 6ft by 6ft or more, flowering first in late June with white single blooms, delicately veined on the petals and with golden stamens. They come in clusters, with blush-pink pointed buds, and the flowers are followed by orange-red, tomato-shaped heps of considerable size. In the autumn these blend in well with the rich gold of the turning foliage. Not the best Rugosa there is, but useful where a large, leafy screen is needed in a very big garden.

Belle Pointevine: 1894. This one would make a rather more restrained hedge or screen, for which it is very suitable, as it only grows to about 5ft, spreading out about the same distance if left to fend for itself. The large, semi-double and rather loosely-formed purplish-pink blooms first appear in early June and are not as strongly scented as most of the family. They open flat and have creamy stamens. Very beautiful, but there are usually only a few orange-red heps to follow.

Blanc Double de Coubert: 1892. Certainly the best of the white Rugosas and one stocked by many nurseries, so that it is easy to get hold of. It forms a 6ft by 5ft shrub, more open, particularly at the base, than most of the others, with fine, fresh green foliage, which is pretty well disease-proof like most of the family. The 4in semi-double and rather loosely formed flowers are very sweetly scented and of the purest papery-white imaginable, set off by buff anthers. They are not particularly rain-proof, but as I said earlier on, they open in succession with such freedom that the spoiling of a few does not matter too much. Matters can be helped if sodden petals are removed from the clusters after heavy rain so that they do not damage the buds to follow. Heps form, but they do not often mature and so they need not be removed to ensure continuity of bloom. AM 1895.

Conrad Ferdinand Meyer: The names certainly do not get any better, do they? This one applies to a huge, 8 to 10ft, very thorny bush, which can if left unchecked spread to almost as much across after some years. It has glossy, dark, leathery foliage, which is subject to black spot and, in some areas, to rust. It can very soon become bare at the base and hard pruning is not really the answer and can be an extremely painful undertaking. Grow it up behind other shrubs and it can be seen in all its magnificence, though you might not think that it had any from what I have said so far. But I haven't described the flowers. It is one of the earliest roses into bloom with a truly breathtaking crop of 4½in silvery-pink double flowers of the Hybrid Tea type, though perhaps a little blowzy by modern standards. The display seems to go on and on, but there is some slackening off before it comes again in September. It is best if given some support, perhaps by growing it against a frame or fence at the back of a border. If not it can be very unruly and in a wind the strong canes with their fearsome thorns can rub against each other and cause serious damage. If you wish, some of the outer branches can be pegged or tied down to hide the gauntness of the lower half. This should certainly be done if it is grown on a pillar. AM 1901. Introduced 1899. Nova Zembla is a white-flowered sport, not quite so vigorous, but otherwise similar.

Fimbriata: 1891. Possibly a cross with a polyantha rose, the clusters of pink flowers have the edges of the petals serrated like a pink. They are semi-double and open flat, and are larger and paler pink than those of Pink Grootendorst, with which it could be compared. They are scented as well, which is another item on the plus side, though I would say that they are not as profuse or continuous. A 5ft by 4ft bush which gained its AM in 1896. Also known as Phoebe's Frilled Pink.

F. J. Grootendorst: 1918. Can form a very tall, rather open (for a Rugosa) bush up to 8ft by 6ft, but it can be kept to 5 or 6ft by pruning and suffer no harm from it. The scentless clusters of flowers, which come with great freedom and very continuously from June onwards, are of a rich crimson, small individually, but there are often upwards of a dozen per spray. The edges of the

PLATE 17

Hybrid Musk roses   page

1. Pax	118
2. Penelope	118
3. Pink Prosperity	119
4. Prosperity	119
5. Thisbe	119
6. Vanity	119
7. Wilhelm	119
8. Will Scarlet	120

<table>
<tr><td>1</td><td>2</td><td>3</td></tr>
<tr><td>4</td><td>5</td><td>6</td></tr>
<tr><td>7</td><td></td><td>8</td></tr>
</table>

petals are serrated in true Grootendorst fashion. Rugosa foliage but on the small side. Very healthy. No heps and needs no dead-heading.

Frau Dagmar Hastrup: is not the best of spellers and does not even know how to spell her own name. Sometimes you see it as Hartopp and I have seen it as Hastrop, though I suspect that in the latter case it was the compiler of that particular catalogue who was the culprit. But whatever name you get it under, it is very well worth while and is one of the more compact Rugosas. It grows to about 5ft by 4ft and will make an excellent 4ft hedge with clipping in the winter. It starts into flower early and has large, 3½in, single, pale pink blooms which have delicate veinings on the petals and creamy-yellow stamens. This is a single-flowered Rugosa and has about the finest heps of the family, which are tomato-shaped and of a rich crimson. The usual good foliage. AM 1958. AGM 1958.

Max Graf: 1919. One case where a rose has not been classed with

1	**2**	**3**
4	**5**	**6**
7	**8**	**9**

PLATE 18

Modern Shrub roses	*page*
1. Aloha	121
2. Ballerina	121
3. Berlin	121
4. Bonn	122
5. Chinatown	122
6. Clair Matin	122
7. Constance Spry	122
8. Dorothy Wheatcroft	123
9. Dortmund	123

the parent it most resembles, for this is a hybrid with a rambler rose and looks and behaves much more like one, except that it spreads naturally along the ground rather than up a tree, though it can be trained to go upwards. There are plenty of other roses for that, though. The leaves resemble those of a rambler and are smooth and glossy. They form an excellent background for the many clusters of 2in single, pink flowers, which pale to white at the base of the petals and have golden stamens. These appear all along the sprawling canes in mid- to late June and continue for a considerable period, though there is no repeat. Best suited for hiding an unsightly bank, where it can ramble at will. AM 1964.

Pink Grootendorst: A 1923 sport of F. J. Grootendorst and very similar to it, except that it is perhaps not quite so vigorous and the flowers are bright pink and, I think, much more attractive. Occasionally the odd branch will revert to the dark red of the parent. AM 1953.

Roseraie de l'Hay: 1901. Undoubtedly one of the finest of the Rugosas if you have room for it, for it will make an 8ft by 8ft shrub in time, densely clothed right to the ground with healthy, bright green foliage on which I have never seen a trace of disease and which turns an attractive yellow in the autumn. The clusters of semi-double flowers begin to appear early in June and the bush is seldom without them from then until the end of September or even later. They are of the most rich-looking wine-red, really sumptuous, but they are rarely followed by heps. Will make a pretty big hedge or impenetrable screen for a pretty big garden. The individual flowers do not last very long, but there always seem to be more to come.

Sarah van Fleet: 1926. Rather resembles Conrad F. Meyer in its habit of growth, in that it is very tall and likely to be bare at the base, though it is probably the more bushy of the two. It should be used in the same ways, i.e., for planting behind other lower-growing shrubs or border plants, and if planted 3ft apart will make a hedge that nothing on earth can get through. For this it is best to prune it in spring to about 4 ft, when it will send up 2–3ft stems, each bearing many clusters of its large, semi-double, cupped but rather loosely formed, warm rose-pink flowers which open to show creamy stamens. The main flushes are in June and September, but in a mild autumn it will go on blooming well into October. Rich scent and will tolerate some shade. AM 1962.

Scabrosa: Growing to about 4ft by 5ft, bushing out well, Scabrosa has the largest flowers of all the single Rugosas. They are some 4–5in in diameter with delicate-looking petals of a soft, fuchsia pink and yellow stamens. One of the first into leaf every year and has particularly good foliage. 1½in tomato-red heps. AM 1964. Sweet scent, weather resistance, fair.

Schneezwerg: 1912. From late May or early June until November this rose is rarely out of flower, the 2½in blooms resembling those of a Japanese anemone, being semi-double, opening flat, white, and with a boss of golden stamnes. They come in clusters of varying size. It makes a dense, twiggy and shapely shrub about 4ft by 5ft, with plenty of small, shiny leaves. It spreads out rather widely, so allowance should be made for this when planting. Small orange heps appear with the later flowers if no dead-heading has been done. It is also known as Snow Dwarf and Snow Sprite, but not very often, unfortunately. Good scent and fair weather resistance. AM 1948.

CHAPTER 14

The Hybrid Musk Roses

A CONSIDERABLE number of roses, mainly fairly similar in habit of growth and flower, was raised by the Rev. Joseph Pemberton early in this century. He called them Hybrid Musk Roses, though the old Musk Rose was a long way back in their pedigree and all that most of them retained of it was its scent. They are marvellous garden shrubs and most of them can be kept within bounds for a small garden by medium pruning in the winter. What is needed is the treatment that you would give to a vigorous floribunda, to which they can be likened in many ways, but the smallest, Danae, does not even need this. At least not to keep it to size.

Lightly pruned, or unpruned except for the cutting away now and then of old wood, most of them will form large, spreading bushes with a tremendous show of bloom in huge trusses in June and July, followed by a period of intermittent flowering during which it is best to remove the old flower heads, and then an even more spectacular show follows in the autumn. They are very healthy and I have never seen disease on any of the Pemberton varieties, though some of the more modern ones descended from them may not be quite so proof.

All the early Hybrid Musks are in shades or mixtures of apricot, cream, pink, pale yellow or white. It has been said that, whatever colour they start, they all end up white, and there is at least some truth in this for the flowers do tend to fade as they age. They are, none the less, lovely at all stages, and the more recent varieties, raised mainly in Germany where they are used extensively for planting in parks, have broadened the colour range, adding crimson, scarlet and lilac.

If you have plenty of space, Hybrid Musks make splendid informal hedges.

Buff Beauty: 1939. Large clusters of creamy-coloured 2–3in, HT-shaped, scented double flowers early in the season (June), the later blooms taking on a deep apricot yellow, paling slightly at the edges. Spreading, arching and rather lax in habit, this will make a 6ft by 7ft bush with rather dark, reddish-green stems and purple-tinted foliage. Good continuity of bloom. Can be used as a pillar rose. AGM.

Cornelia: With Penelope, probably the best known of the Hybrid Musks, and almost always in flower from June onwards. The salmon-pink buds, in large and small trusses, open to rosette-type blooms of strawberry pink, flushed yellow, which fade to a coppery pink. Glossy, dark green leaves on a fragrant, wide-spreading bush about 6ft by 7ft. Makes a good hedge, when it can be kept rather smaller and more compact by pruning. 1925. Good in rainy weather.

Danae: 1913. One of the less vigorous ones, making a bush about 4ft by 3ft, with dark green, glossy leaves, but there is no lack of trusses of the semi-double, apricot-yellow flowers, which fade in time to ivory. The first of the Pemberton varieties. AM 1912.

Felicia: 1928. Lower growing and more spreading than most (though not so small as Danae), but still reasonably compact and bushy, it makes a 5ft by 6–7ft shrub, good for a hedge or for bedding if suitably pruned. Large clusters of 3in, HT-type blooms in two tones of china and salmon-pink, the colour deepening in the centre of the flowers. Strong fragrance and especially good in the autumn. AGM 1965.

Francesca: Dark red wood and glossy leaves on a vigorous 6ft by 6ft plant with rather loosely-shaped flowers of apricot yellow, fading to cream and sweetly scented. 1922.

Hamburg: One of the more modern Hybrid Musks, not one of the Pemberton group, and erect in growth, more like a tall floribunda. It starts into flower in mid- to late June with large trusses of semi-double crimson-scarlet flowers which have darker tones blending in, contrasting vividly with the yellow stamens. Rather scanty foliage low down as it does not bush out much below 3ft, so it is best grown at the back of a border. Slight scent. 6ft by 3–4ft. 1935.

Magenta: 1954. Another comparatively modern one that does not conform to the Hybrid Musk pattern. It has long, 4ft, lax canes with clusters of flowers coming mainly at or near the ends, and weighing them down to the ground if not given support. The flowers themselves are very lovely, sweetly scented and very double, opening flat and sometimes quartered like the old roses. They are in the most delicate tones of rosy lilac, so that the variety is most unfortunately named. They also come in rather tight clusters, which tend to prevent the petals of spent blooms from falling cleanly and it is really necessary to remove these by hand, especially after heavy rain, which can make them into a sodden mess and ruin unopened buds underneath. Some mildew and black spot possible. Rather sparse, dark green foliage. Not one of my first choices in shrub roses, but many speak so highly of it that I did not feel I should leave it out.

Moonlight: 1913. Lemon-yellow in the bud, the semi-double flowers come in enormous trusses on which I have counted up to eighty flowers, especially in the autumn. They are ivory-white, fading to pure white, and have yellow stamens and a rich fragrance. Dark red stems and dark green leaves on a very robust grower to 6 or 7ft (taller if used on a pillar) by 4–5ft. AM 1913.

Pax: Another large bush, 6ft by 6ft, more lax and arching than Moonlight, and with the largest flowers of all the Hybrid Musks. They are semi-double and of a waxy white, with a hint of yellow in the centre and large golden stamens. Strong scent. 1918.

Penelope: the flowers, which come in small trusses and much larger ones of twenty to thirty flowers, are a lovely blend of cream, coppery pink, and with sometimes a hint of pale yellow. They are semi-double and rather loosely formed, opening first in June and from then almost continuous, but with usually an even bigger autumn display in September/October. They are followed by attractive but not particularly showy greyish-pink heps. A very rugged grower to 6ft by 5ft, branching widely from low down and with good, glossy leaves. Can be used for bedding. AGM 1956.

Pink Prosperity: Dark leaves and dark red stems on a sturdy, rather upright, 5ft by 4ft bush. The large trusses have small, double, scented flowers of a clear, bright pink, fading paler but produced very freely. They are at their most perfect at the half-open stage. A sport from Prosperity and not quite so vigorous. Strong fragrance. 1931.

Prosperity: 1919. Similar to Pink Prosperity, but probably reaching 7ft and with flowers a blend of cream and pink, fading white.

Thisbe: 1918. A good one for bedding, for with no bullying from the secateurs it only reaches 4ft by 4ft. The richly scented blooms are semi-double, opening into rosettes of buff-yellow, fading to cream. They have amber stamens. Lighter green leaves than most of the family.

Vanity: 1920. The only single-flowered Hybrid Musk and distinctive in other ways as well. It will easily reach 8 or 9ft and is even more prone than others of the group to send out enormous rigid branches at unexpected angles, crowned with immense corymbs of deep rose-pink flowers, lighter in the autumn, which have a sweet but not strong perfume. Not over-blessed with leaves, it is often recommended that three or four should be planted together about a yard apart (if you have room for a group that will be at the very least 15ft across), when it will make a most spectacular display. As the habit of growth is taller and also unpredictable, it is not advisable to mix it with other Hybrid Musks in a hedge planting. AM 1956. FCC 1958.

Wilhelm: Introduced in 1934, this is one of the non-Pemberton Musks, a very robust and rather upright grower, reaching 7ft (or 10ft on a pillar) by 5ft. Only slightly fragrant, it blooms very freely with trusses of 3in, semi-double, crimson flowers which are slightly lighter towards the centre and have golden stamens. The colour fades somewhat in strong sunlight and can take on a bluish tinge. Medium-sized red heps follow them. Almost thornless.

Will Scarlet: This sported from Wilhelm in 1948 and is similar except for the colour of the flowers which are lighter and more nearly approaching scarlet, again with the paling off towards the centre. AM 1954.

CHAPTER 15

Modern Shrub Roses

THESE are such a diverse lot that I cannot really generalise about them as I have with the other groups. They include short climbers grown as shrubs, hybrids bred on purpose to resemble some of the old roses, extra large floribundas and extra large Hybrid Teas. So all I can do is to describe each one as fully as possible, making any special point there may be about it and including notes on pruning for each where there is a divergence from the normal. There are modern shrub roses for every garden.

Aloha: 1949. Usually sold as a climber, in which form it will reach 10ft, though rather slowly, and in my experience it is one of the most truly recurrent there is, with two main flushes in June/July and again in September/October, with quite a good show in between. As a 6ft by 4ft shrub it is equally good, with first-rate, glossy and completely healthy foliage, setting off perfectly the small clusters of large, very double, warm pink, scented flowers, which have a deeper colour at the heart and are completely rain-proof. They grow on long stems and are perfect for cutting. Little pruning is needed other than the occasional shortening of the side growths from the main stems in winter. It may need some support once it reaches full size.

Ballerina: 1937. A vigorous, spreading, 5ft by 6ft bush with abundant, small, glossy, light green leaves, which are very resistant to disease. It is recurrent, with a very good autumn performance, when it will be covered with masses of small, single, apple-blossom-pink flowers which have a white eye and which fade paler. It will be covered with them in the summer, too, of course. They come in large trusses and are very rain-resistant. Can be used for bedding if you have plenty of space.

Berlin: 1949. Large trusses, intermittently produced, of $3\frac{1}{2}$in single orange-scarlet flowers of great brilliance but with very little scent. An upright 4ft by 3ft shrub with the habit of a large floribunda, large dark green leaves and distinctive red thorns. TGC 1950.

Bonn: 1950. One to grow behind others as it tends to be leggy and will reach 6ft by 4ft. The leaves are glossy, large, light green and leathery, and the flowers, which are about 3in in diameter, are a mixture of deep salmon and orange-scarlet, which may fade in time to a not too attractive purplish tint. They are double, but rather loosely formed and can be rather shapeless. Little scent, though this is a descendant of the Hybrid Musks. It needs dead-heading if a long flowering season is to be achieved, but will produce large, deep-red heps in the autumn. AM 1962. CM 1950.

Buff Beauty: See p. 117.

Chinatown: 1963. A very robust, upright grower to 5ft or so, which will bush out to 3–4ft and be well covered with very attractive bright green glossy foliage. I have heard it said that it spends more time making leaves than flowers, but this has not been my experience. Mine bear, in June and July, and again in September and October, many trusses, each with up to seven or eight very large, weather-proof, 4in and double, clear bright yellow flowers, sometimes with just a hint of pink about them. Individually, they are not unlike smaller and more strongly coloured versions of the blooms of Peace, but they are very sweetly scented, which the latter are not. I have only once seen black spot on the leaves and never mildew. Makes a very good hedge. Prune lightly as for a tall-growing floribunda. FCC 1967. GM 1962.

Clair Matin: 1961. Large and small clusters of medium-sized semi-double, light flesh-pink flowers which open to show golden stamens and have a sweet scent. The light green foliage on the 5ft by 7ft bush is sometimes crimson tinted and is healthy on the whole. Makes a good hedge and is more recurrent than perpetual in bloom.

Constance Spry: This will make a very large, well rounded bush, probably 7ft by 7ft, the leaves coppery tinted when young, changing to dark green. Some of the more lax branches may need some support from surrounding shrubs, and all of them will bear along almost their entire length double flowers which can be as much as 6in across. They come in heads of several together and are very fragrant, cupped in shape, and are of a clear rose-pink. One of the best of the modern shrubs in the old pattern, and like them, once-flowering only, starting early in June and carrying on over a long period with great enthusiasm. Makes a good pillar rose as well as being grown as a shrub. AM 1965. Introduced 1961.

Dorothy Wheatcroft: Also from 1961, this is really a very tall and rather gaunt-growing floribunda, which needs to be placed behind something else to get the best out of it – and that best is very good. It bears huge clusters of semi-double, 3in flowers officially described as orient red, but as I am not really sure what that is, I prefer to say scarlet with deeper shadings. They make a spectacular show, though they can take on a slightly purplish-pink tinge with age. The petals have scalloped edges and have good rain resistance, but there is only the slightest of scents. Glossy, medium-green leaves which are very healthy. AM 1960. GM 1961. Good repeat flowering, and good weather resistance. 4–5ft.

Dortmund: 1955. Generally sold as a pillar rose, this will, if given some support, make a very good, freely branching and slightly lax shrub with dark, glossy, pointed leaves. As a climber it will reach 8ft and as a shrub 5ft by 8ft, arching wide and bearing trusses of very large (4in) single crimson-red flowers with a most distinctive white eye and buff-yellow stamens. These are only fully recurrent if the old trusses are removed after the first flush.

Elmshorn: 1950. 5–6ft tall and about the same across, this makes a well-branched bush which needs a distinct rest between the first flush of bloom in June and July and the second in September and October. The 1½in flowers are fully double, cup-shaped, come in large trusses, and are of a brilliant deep carmine-pink, which is difficult to mix with other roses. No noticeable scent. Small, dark, glossy leaves. Can be grown on a pillar.

Erfurt: 1939. Clear, rose-pink, semi-double flowers freely produced in clusters and having white centres often tinted pale primrose and with a very prominent boss of deep golden stamens. The bush is spreading and arching, building up to about 5ft by 6ft, the leaves having a coppery tint when young, which is most attractive. They are healthy and the bush is in flower through most of the summer. Scented.

First Choice: 1958. An extra vigorous floribunda, reaching 5ft by 4ft after a year or two if not too heavily pruned. It bears, when they are newly opened, some of the most spectacular flowers of any rose. They are single but enormous, some 4½in across, with butterfly-like petals in the brightest orange-scarlet, shading to yellow in the centre and with a pale, yellowish-pink reverse. This reverse colouring often shows prominently in the truss and forms a most striking contrast to the fiery shades of the face of the flowers, but strangely it rarely, if ever, gets a mention in rose catalogues. Unfortunately the blooms age a rather ugly dark pinkish-red so that they should be removed from the trusses as this begins to happen, or the whole effect will be spoiled. So it is not a rose for the lazy gardener. Reasonable rain resistance and fragrance. The bush is well branched from very low down with plum red canes and has dark green foliage which is not quite mildew-proof. Prune as for a floribunda. CM 1958.

Fred Loads: Raised by an amateur in 1967, this will, I believe, go up to 7ft by about 3 to 4ft, but I have never seen it as big as this. My own, about three years old, have so far reached 4ft by 4ft as vigorous, fairly upright but well branched shrubs with plentiful and pleasing light green, semi-glossy leaves, that seem very healthy. The flowers, which come in trusses which can exceed eighteen inches in width, are some 4in in diameter, single, and of the most lovely light vermilion-orange, paling a little towards the centre and sweetly scented. Can be used for large beds or for a low hedge – or a tall one if it does go up to 7ft – if it is not grown as a specimen or in a group of three or four. Prune as for a large floribunda. AM 1967. GM 1967.

Frensham: 1946. I have hesitated before including this large and very vigorous floribunda, as it seems to be deteriorating and in many cases (my own included and I have, in fact, got rid of it) it has become a martyr to mildew. On the other hand this experience, though fairly general, is not by any means universal. Many people still swear by this rose as a very colourful one, almost always in flower, suitable for a large bed or for a fairly upright but well branched 4ft hedge, so I am putting it in my list and leaving it to you to decide whether it is worth taking a chance. The 3in flowers are semi-double and of a deep, glowing scarlet-crimson, rather loosely formed, and come in heads of varying sizes but many of them large and showy. They are good in the rain, but with little, if any, scent. Fine, glossy, mid-green leaves and large thorns. One of the best floribundas ever produced and it is a great pity that it has developed problems in its old age. GM 1944.

Fritz Nobis: 1940. Once-flowering only from mid-June, but with a tremendous display that lasts for many weeks. The 4in semi-double, scented blooms resemble those of a Hybrid Tea, and are of a soft salmon-pink with darker shadings and weigh down the branches with their profusion. The bush is rounded and full, about 6ft by 6ft, and has glossy, leathery leaves and dark red, rounded heps in the autumn. One of the very best, and makes a wonderful specimen shrub. AM 1959.

Frühlingsanfang: See p. 73.

Frühlingsgold: See p. 74.

Frühlingsmorgen: See p. 74.

Frühlingsduft: See p. 74.

Goldbush: A 5ft by 6ft rose, equally good as a shrub, when it will spread out wide, or on a pillar, and with glossy, light green leaves. Mid- to late-June flowering, it has attractive, salmon-flushed buds, opening to semi-double blooms in a mixture of peach-pink and pale yellow and with golden stamens. Scented. AM 1965.

Golden Chersonese: 1963. This should, I suppose, have been included amongst the species roses, but why should I not add my own small contribution to the general confusion over classification? It is a modern cross between R. *ecae* and Canarybird (described in Chapter 5), which it resembles in many ways, though the bright yellow single flowers are smaller and of a more intense colour than the latter, but bigger than the former. Like them both, it is spring-flowering only, starting in late May, and forms a bushy, twiggy, upright, 6ft by 7ft shrub with small but plentiful dainty leaves. Some scent. AM 1966. TGC 1969. CM 1970.

Golden Moss: Although this was introduced in 1932, it follows the pattern of growth of the old Moss Roses, except in the colour of its double, canary-yellow blooms, which rather rapidly fade except in the heart of the flower to a creamy yellow. It is always a bit of a surprise to see a Moss in this colour and it takes a little getting used to if you are accustomed to the more traditional ones. Dark green leaves and dark green moss on a 6ft by 6ft lax-growing shrub, which is recurrent, though the first blooming in June is by far the best.

Golden Wings: 1956. This is classed officially as a Hybrid Tea, though only a botanist could presumably tell you why, as it certainly does not resemble one. The flowers are very large and single (yes, I do know that there were some single Hybrid Teas in the 1920s and 1930s) and come in medium-sized clusters on a 5ft fairly upright bush which will, in time, branch out to about the same distance. They are pale yellow, deepening towards the centre, and with amber stamens, all together rather like the flowers of the climber, Mermaid. The bush is never out of flower from mid-June onwards, though I would put it in the beautiful rather than the spectacularly profuse class. Quality and very fair quantity. I remove heps to help with continuity of bloom. The matt, light green leaves are seemingly disease-proof and are rather long and pointed. Cut back old, worn out branches occasionally and shorten the others by about one-third. This is the rose where I differ with authority as to its suitability for light soils. My answer is an emphatic Yes. AM 1965.

Gruss an Aachen: 1909. One for the small garden or for bedding generally, as it only grows to about 2ft 6in, spreading out to about the same. It bears a mass of large (4–5in), scented, creamy flesh-pink flowers which fade somewhat and are very double, opening flat. Rich green leaves, which need watching for mildew. Perpetual.

Hamburg: See p. 117.

Heidelberg: 1958. All the roses in this section which are named after German towns, have their origin, not surprisingly, in Germany, and all of them are of exceptional hardiness. Heidelberg is one of them and, 5–6ft by about 4ft, it makes an upright plant with a moderate lateral spread, and with plenty of glossy, bronze-tinted, dark green, healthy leaves. The 3½in flowers come in clusters and are semi-double, only very slightly scented, and of an intense crimson-scarlet, fading slightly. Very showy and hardy and will grow anywhere except in concrete, so that it can be used to introduce a splash of colour into difficult positions in gardens. Good autumn display. Can be used as a pillar rose up to about 7ft. CM 1958. AM 1961.

Hunter: 1960. A 6ft Rugosa hybrid and a profuse bloomer from mid-June and again in the autumn. Bright crimson double flowers in clusters and with HT-like leaves, this is a bushy grower suitable for an informal hedge.

Iceberg: 1958. A top recommendation among the floribundas since its introduction, this can grow, if not severely pruned, into a tall, airy shrub of 6ft or more by about 4ft. The 3in blooms come all over the bush at all levels on the slender branches, in sprays large and small, and in great profusion. Sometimes tinted pink in the bud, they open, camellia-like, to pure white, and are extremely lovely and delicately scented. An enormous flush in June and July, some flowers in August and an extremely impressive autumn show. Unfortunately it can get black spot (though I have never seen it very bad), and there is some tendency to mildew, especially on the foot-stalks of the flowers. It stands rain very well on the whole, though sometimes the flowers can be spotted with pink after a prolonged wetting. Light green, plentiful foliage. GM 1958.

Joseph's Coat: 1963. Can be used as a short climber though its long, strong canes are none too easy to train. As a shrub it will reach 6ft, branching and arching out to 8ft or more in a rather haphazard way, with healthy, abundant, glossy, mid-green leaves. The flowers are prolific in summer, with a rather less spectacular autumn flush and a few in between. Spectacular is indeed the word for this rose in June and July, for it bears large sprays of 3in semi-double blooms in a mixture of gold, orange and cherry-red, shaded and veined a deeper orange. They are only slightly scented. Can be used for an informal hedge with great effect. AM 1966. TGC 1963.

Kassel: 1957. Incredibly massive heads of large, loosely-formed flowers in a mixture of carmine and cherry-red, with a hint of flame but little scent. Perpetually in bloom, the flowers come on a 7ft by 6ft rather lax-growing bush, with dark, glossy, disease-free leaves and reddish canes. A descendant of the Hybrid Musks, it is not dissimilar to, though more vigorous than, its sister German rose, Bonn. First-rate, but needs plenty of room. AM 1964. CM 1957.

PLATE 19

Modern Shrub roses   *page*

1. Elmshorn	123
2. Erfurt	123
3. First Choice	124
4. Fred Loads	124
5. Frensham	125
6. Fritz Nobis	125
7. Goldbush	125
8. Golden Cheronese	125
9. Golden Moss	125

1	2	3
4	5	6
7	8	9

Laughter: 1948. A not very well known but good, vigorous shrub, which will reach 5–6ft by 4ft. It is rather an open grower with clusters of semi-double, cupped blooms of a rich salmon colour with an apricot reverse, the salmon fading to light salmon-pink. Scented, the flowers appear later than most unless the bush is left unpruned – late June or early July is the usual starting time – and they come again in September. Light green leaves, which are usually healthy, and attractive red thorns.

Lavender Lassie: Very large heads of very double 3in blooms of the pompon type with many short petals like a number of the old roses, though this one dates from 1959. The weight of the trusses weighs down the rather slender branches so that they do need some support, but it will grow to 4 or 5ft, the spread depending on how much support is given. Despite its name, I have never been able to detect any lavender colouring in the blooms, which on my specimens are a pure soft rose-pink, fading paler and sweetly though not very powerfully scented. Good, very

PLATE 20

Modern Shrub roses

healthy, light green foliage. Stands rain well for a rose with so many petals.

Magenta: See p. 118.

Maigold: 1953. A big 7ft by 8ft rambling, loose and very thorny shrub or a 15ft climber for a wall or fence. It flowers early in May with a grand display over several weeks and if the dead heads are removed there can be some further, intermittent bloom, though do not count on it. The 3in flowers are semi-double, loosely cupped in shape and bronze-yellow, shading to flesh pink at the edges of the petals, and with crimson, gold-tipped stamens. Good fragrance and medium-green, glossy leaves.

Moyesii Eos: See p. 69.

Moyesii Geranium: See p. 69.

Moyesii Nevada: See p. 70.

Moyesii Marguerite Hilling: See p. 70.

Nymphenburg: 1954. Another large, arching, informal shrub to about 6ft by 6ft, or up to 18ft on a wall if used as a climber. Large double blooms of salmon-pink with golden tints and a yellow base to the petals. Large, dark, glossy leaves. Sweet scent.

Ormiston Roy: See R. *spinosissima* 'Ormiston Roy', p. 73.

Peace: 1945. Probably the most famous Hybrid Tea ever introduced and hardly needing a detailed description. In most cases used as a bedding rose, if lightly pruned (Peace should never be very hard pruned anyway) it will make a 4–6ft specimen or hedge shrub with wonderful, healthy, glossy green leaves and its well-known, huge, pale yellow flowers. Shoots with no flower buds can appear in early summer, but if these are cut back by about one-third to a good side bud, blooms should quite quickly follow. GM 1947.

Pink Prosperity: See p. 119.

Poulsen's Park Rose: 1953. A robust, 5ft by 5ft shrub, with large and small heads of light pink, semi-double, fragrant blooms. Good foliage and deep red canes. Flowers first in June/July with magnificent generosity, rests in August, and gets going once more in September/October. It is not too happy in the rain.

Queen Elizabeth: 1955. Like Peace, a very well-known rose that is seen everywhere, but it is often grown in the wrong place and in the wrong way. It can grow enormously tall (8–9ft) and, if not properly pruned, have most of its lovely, slightly scented, cupped, silvery-pink flowers right at the top. They look marvellous from the upper deck of a bus or from a passing airliner. Naturally a very upright grower, the cutting back by as much as one-half of some of the main shoots to an outward-facing eye each year will help it to bush out in time and produce bloom lower down. The remaining shoots should be pruned as for a floribunda and, if it is treated like this, it can make a wonderful hedge which will take up little lateral space. It is also useful for the back of the border. The flowers come on long stems, singly and in small clusters, and last well when cut. Reasonably good in the rain, but not completely mildew-proof. GM 1955.

Scarlet Fire: Very long, arching branches make this an informal, spreading shrub about 7ft by 7ft, which can also be used as a pillar rose. Once flowering only in July, the blooms, which come in clusters all along the branches, are large, single, and of the most breath-taking flaming scarlet, set off by golden stamens in the centre. They are followed by pear-shaped red heps. The leaves are a matt mid-green. A sensational rose during its rather brief period of glory, and rather surprisingly a hybrid of one of the Gallicas. Introduced in 1952. AM 1960.

Sparrieshoop: 1952. A profuse but intermittent bloomer throughout the summer and autumn, this makes an upright 6ft by 4ft, rather open bush, with clusters of 4in single, salmon-pink flowers and purplish-brown wood and purple tinted leaves. The blooms are scented, but do not age well and must be removed regularly. A parent of Heidelberg.

St Nicholas: See p. 81.

Uncle Walter: 1963. A 5ft and often rather ungainly Hybrid Tea which has its place at the back of the border, where the wonderful and very free, deep crimson-scarlet, high-centred, velvety blooms and leathery, coppery foliage can be admired and the habit of growth concealed. The flowers do not blue with age, as is the case with so many roses of this colour. They have only a slight scent, but if they are at the back of the bed this need only be of concern to Cyrano de Bergerac or Pinocchio. CM 1963.

Wilhelm: See p. 119.

Will Scarlet: See p. 120.

CHAPTER 16

Climbing and Rambling Roses

THE climbers and ramblers listed in the following pages are in the main some of the best, and in some cases the more unusual, that were popular in the time of the Old Roses. There are vast quantities of ramblers from that period or very little later which are still grown and sold widely, as there has been far less development of new varieties in this field than there has been with Hybrid Teas and floribundas. As a nursery sells perhaps one climber to every ten bush roses, there has been less incentive to breed new types, though one or two hybridisers, notably in America and McGredy's and Wilhelm Kordes in Europe, are now working hard to produce climbers that really do flower continuously or at least repeat well. Very few do this at present, whatever the catalogues may say, and the ramblers, of course, never pretended to. A few of the more modern roses are also included in the list.

Nearly all the roses that I describe date from the last century and most of those that do not are either derived from them or have only been rediscovered more recently. All consort well with the Old Roses and most of them are extremely vigorous, suitable for large walls (climbers only unless you like mildew), pergolas, or rambling over old, unsightly sheds or up into trees. Several of them have huge – and I do mean huge – heads of hundreds of flowers so tiny that it is difficult to believe that they are roses, though the scent leaves one in little doubt. Two of them, *banksiae lutea* and *brunonii* La Mortala are not too hardy, except in a sheltered spot in the southern counties. Most are once-flowering. Unless you really have room for them, choose very carefully, or you may have to fight your way out of your front door after a few years.

Aimée Vibert: A 15ft rambler introduced in 1828, with very shiny dark green leaves and fragrant white flowers quite early in

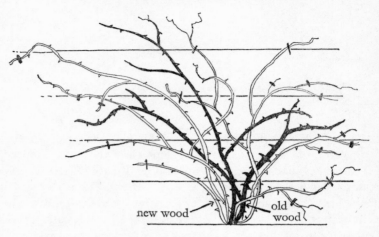

Pruning a rambler. Cut old wood to ground level.
Tie in and tip new wood

June and a few later if you are lucky. One of the more restrained growers.

Albéric Barbier: 1900. A rampant rambler to 15ft or so, for fences, trellis or pergolas and just about the healthiest rambler there is. The foliage is plentiful (a great advantage in a rambler or climber, this, as it will not look leggy), small, dark green with sometimes a bronze tint, is glossy, and it stays on the plant well into the winter. The small yellow buds open to double, creamy-white flowers with a pointed centre. They fade almost to white with age, are fragrant, and are produced with great profusion in small clusters in early June, with a few flowers later. This rose is an exception to the general rule about rambler pruning which says that all old canes should be cut back to the base each year. The blooms of Albéric Barbier come on the side shoots of the previous year's wood, so prune as for a climber rather than a rambler.

Albertine: 1921. An extremely vigorous (15ft) rambler which can be grown in a number of ways, on a wall, fence, pergola, or as a rather unruly weeping standard, in which form it is often sold. Or, if given some support, it can make a great, sprawling bush which in June and July will become a huge mound of blossom,

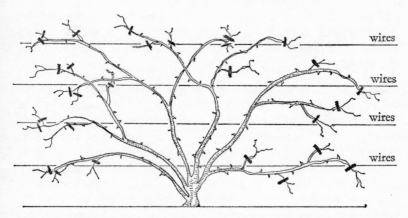

Pruning a climber and ramblers like Albertina and Albéric Barbier.
Only cut back side shoots to one or two eyes – or do not prune at all!

sending out waves of scent into the air around. The flowers are large for a rambler, copper-pink in the bud, and a soft pink with a high centre when opened, fading a little in hot sunshine. Prolonged heavy rain can leave the petals a rather soggy mess, though the odd shower will do little harm and normally the petals will drop cleanly when the blossoms fade. The foliage is coppery to dark green, shiny, but unfortunately does take some mildew, though not usually till well after flowering time, for there is no repeat bloom after the first flush. The new growths are a striking dark red.

As I mentioned, Albertine is in many growers' lists as a weeping standard, but it really does not take naturally to this form of treatment. The very strong canes are comparatively stiff and do not weep without a good deal of assistance. It takes a lot of training to get them to hang down evenly all round, as would a rose like Crimson Shower, and it will be constantly rebelling and shooting off in all directions. But if you do not mind a rather unbalanced and very sweetly scented waterfall of pink down one side, and a good deal less at the other, Albertine is your rose. It certainly is mine, but do use a very strong stake.

Albertine is another exception to the rambler pruning rule, as it flowers on the old wood as well as the new. I simply cut out the odd bit of dead wood that occurs from time to time and remove any adventurous cane that decides to obstruct a rather narrow path that runs near the one I grow as a shrub. It thrives on this treatment.

Alister Stella Gray: 1894. An old favourite, growing to 15ft, with its orange-yellow buds, which come in small clusters, opening into small, creamy-yellow flowers which are richly fragrant. There seem to be very conflicting views as to whether this rose has a good repeat performance in the autumn and I have never grown it myself and only seen it in bloom in June. I suppose the answer is that it does repeat if it is in the right situation and would probably be helped by dead-heading as well. Mr Graham Thomas describes "huge new shoots with large heads of bloom in the autumn" and he should know. At its best trained against an old, mellowed, brick wall.

Banksiae lutea: 1824. The double yellow form of *R. banksiae*, the Banksian Rose, which is white and was introduced from China in 1807. *Banksiae lutea* is probably the more popular and is an extremely vigorous rambler which needs to be grown in deep, rich soil and on a warm south wall or all the flowering shoots will be killed by frost. No pruning should be done or you will lose them that way instead, by cutting them off. Plant it and leave it alone, except for training. The rose is thornless, or nearly so, with light green, glossy leaves which will last well into the winter. As it will grow to 25ft or so it needs plenty of space. The bright yellow double flowers come in clusters in May and early June and make a wonderful show. AM 1960.

Brunonii La Mortala: Probably a form of the old Musk Rose, though only introduced in 1954, this rambler is ideal for growing up trees, when it will reach 25ft, or scrambling over a wall, though only in warm districts, for it is not completely hardy. Trusses of 1in creamy-white flowers with golden stamens in July and true Musk fragrance. They are not too good in a wet summer. A very fast grower.

Casino: 1963. One of the newer climbers and a good repeat

flowerer, with two main flushes and a few blooms in between. These are medium-sized, double, and of a pleasing soft yellow, stand wet weather well and do not fade. There is some scent, but it is not strong. It is a vigorous, well-branched plant going up to about 15ft, with generally healthy light to mid-green foliage, though mine has had mildew occasionally in a mild way. Like some other climbers, I have found it to be a slow starter, taking two years to settle down and get under way. But nothing is wrong with its performance after that. GM 1963.

Cécile Brunner, Climbing: 1904. This, the climbing version of the small shrub described in Chapter 10, is by contrast a very vigorous climber, going to 20ft or so, though taking a while to do so. It has good, red-tinted, rather pointed leaves and slightly larger versions of the tiny pink flowers of the bush form. A profuse bloomer in June and into July, only the odd spray or two will appear later.

Chaplin's Pink Climber: 1928. The name is misleading as this is a rambler and not a climber, and to make things even more confusing it does not shoot up very much from the base as a rambler should – or at least my one does not. It grows like a vigorous climber up an old and more or less dead pear tree, sending out new shoots regularly from quite high up and flowering profusely on the old wood. Climbers and ramblers are quite maddening in their inconsistency, but in this case it is just as well, as the pear tree would be quite unsafe to put a ladder up against to disentangle old canes each year. Chaplin's Pink flowers only once, though over many weeks, with large clusters of medium-sized, semi-double blooms of a very strong pink, which is not everybody's favourite. In fact I am not sure that it is mine, but isolated as it is up a tree it does not clash with anything else, and it gives a colourful display. No mildew or black spot. In general, this rose is very similar to the old favourite the American Pillar rose, but without the white eye and with a rather softer pink.

Danse du Feu: (Syn. Spectacular) 1954. This orange-red climber received tremendous publicity when it first appeared and it is now in nearly every nursery list. From my own experience I would say that it is overrated. The first flush of bloom is certainly a dazzling colour, but the petals all too rapidly lose their glow and turn to an unattractive, rather dirty red. It did pretty well during a recent exceptionally fine and hot summer, but generally if there is anything in the way of prolonged rain, the petals stick together and do not fall cleanly. The blooms form brown, sodden lumps all over the plant, rather as if someone had been flicking spoonfuls of burnt porridge at it, and as it goes up to 12ft to 15ft, it is none too easy to do anything about them. Mine grows on a wall and fairly bad mildew has sometimes spoiled the later flowers. It is recommended for walls, but perhaps is less prone to mildew and a little black spot on a fence or pillar, where it can get more air.

Easlea's Golden Rambler: 1932. Often known simply as Golden Rambler, this is a vigorous grower up to 10ft, with stiff, very branched canes and dark green, glossy foliage. The flowers have some fragrance and come in small trusses. There is a first flush and some repeat later, but by no means as profuse. The blooms are of medium size and a good bright yellow with irregular red splashes on the outsides of the petals. Generally healthy, it grows well on a wall, pillar or rose arch.

Elegance: 1937. Enormously vigorous, this grows up to 15 or 20ft and mine covers half the front of my house, sending out new long canes every year so that I am beginning to wonder when it will stop. It is covered from the end of May to the end of June with very large, beautifully shaped primrose blooms, which shade to a deeper yellow at the heart and are equal in size and form to the best of the Hybrid Teas, and of exhibition standard. They grow on long stems, which makes them good for cutting, though they do not last more than about two days in water. Mildew and a little black spot can be a problem, but not so bad that it cannot be controlled by spraying, even if you have to do the top from the bedroom windows. Mid-green, slightly glossy foliage. Once flowering only, which may make some people hesitate, but I think it is one of the loveliest climbers of all.

Emily Gray: 1918. This rambler will grow up to 15ft and has medium to large, double, buff-yellow flowers in trusses, opening from yellow buds. It is summer flowering only, but the very dark green, glossy and healthy foliage, with its large leaves, looks most handsome after the blooms have gone. It is said to be subject to die-back, but I have never found this to be so.

Félicité et Perpétue: 1827. Still to be seen on old cottages, where it may well have been growing since its introduction. If you can beg a cutting, take one, for it will root easily. It is, as you will have gathered, a very tough and hardy rambler, which will keep its dark green leaves for at least nine months of the year and bears in July in clusters of varying size, 1½in blush-white flowers with hundreds of small petals which open to small pompons. I say hundreds, but actually I have never counted the petals of a rose that has more than Mermaid, by which time I have generally found out that she loves me, so why go on? The flowers are not strongly scented. Probably 12–15ft, with long slim branches that are easy to train, it is good on a pillar, or it can be grown as a rather sprawling, low bush. Good weather resistance. Only cut out old, dead wood as necessary and tip back flowering shoots.

Filipes Kiftsgate: An enormous rambler through, and taker-over of, trees, needing very strong support, and smothered in late June and July in huge heads of many tiny (½in) creamy-white flowers with yellow stamens and a rich fragrance. Reaches 20 to 30 ft and spreads wide in all directions like a floral explosion. From Western China. 1954.

Garland, The: 1835. A sweetly scented rambler with large clusters of semi-double blush-pink blooms which fade quite rapidly to white and are followed by small red heps. A favourite of Miss Jekyll (if you care) and her advice was to get up at 4 a.m. in mid-June to admire the newly-opened buds. I've never seen them. 15ft.

Gloire de Dijon: This old climber, raised in 1853, has a number of distinctions. It is one of the earliest of all into flower, in most years in the first half of May, and from then on it is more continuously in bloom than almost any other rose, old or new. It is also one of the very earliest roses with Hybrid Tea-type flowers to have distinct yellowish tones, though actually it is more buff than yellow, with a touch also of apricot. The 4in flowers are very double and with rather muddled petals by the standards of modern large-flowered roses. Some blooms are quartered and all are very sweetly scented. Recommended for a wall, on which it will reach 15ft. Best with no pruning, but if it gets out of hand or bare at the base, the stoutest canes can be shortened to 6–8ft and the medium ones to 4–6ft. Certain breeding stock of this rose is believed to be deteriorating, presumably through over propagation over many years from bad initial specimens. This makes it particularly important to order from a reliable nursery if you are to get good plants.

Golden Showers: 1956. One of the very best of the (sometimes) short climbers which is often catalogued as a shrub. It is bright yellow, seems to be quite disease-free and really does stay in bloom all the summer. There is a main flush in June and another in August/September, but there are plenty of flowers in between as well. They have long, elegant buds but not a great many petals, so that eventually they open flat and then fall cleanly. They stand up to rain well and, growing on long, practically thornless stems, are good for cutting and last quite well in water. The leaves are dark green and glossy. In most descriptions I have read of this rose it is said to grow to about 8ft and to be ideal for a pillar or as a rather upright shrub. I do not know if I am especially lucky with climbers, or whether they simply do not like me and are trying to get away over the roof, but with me Golden Showers, growing on a wall, goes happily up to 15ft with flowers from the top to the bottom, and it is not the only variety that does more than it apparently should.

Goldfinch: A 10ft rambler of 1907 for pillars, pergolas or to be grown as an informal 6–7ft shrub. The clusters of strongly scented, semi-double flowers are yellow, fading to cream, and come in late June or early in July with no repeat. This, together with Veilchenblau (which see) is of a form of rambler which does not always make new wood from the base, and old stems should not be cut out if there are none to replace them. Not too many flowers on an old stem are better than none at all, but if vigorous new stems branch out from higher up the old ones, these can be shortened by about one-third in February. AM 1907.

Handel: 1965. One of the most successful repeat-flowering climbers to have been introduced in recent years and unique in colouring for a large-flowered climber. The double blooms are blush-white, with the most attractive carmine shading to the petal edges. Vigorous up to 15ft with good, healthy, glossy, mid-green foliage. The flowers stand wet weather well. TGC 1965.

Lawrence Johnston: A very vigorous climber, going up to 20ft, though it took three years for mine to really get moving. It is now up to about 15ft in an old apple tree, but I have seen this rose literally covering the wall of a large house. The bright green, glossy leaves set off well the bright yellow flowers, which are of medium size and cup-shaped when newly open. After a little while they fade slightly and become rather loosely formed, though without losing their attraction or their scent. It makes a colourful show in June, but only occasionally will there be a few flowers later. Quite an old rose, but only put into commerce comparatively recently. AM 1948.

Longiscuspis: What a name for a lovely rose from Western China and the Himalayas! It is like *filipes* Kiftsgate in many ways and better for cold districts and ones with difficult soils – even for chalk. It has very glossy leaves, is late flowering, in August, at which time it is almost hidden by the many heads of tiny, single, white flowers, which are strongly scented. This is one of the ones which people need convincing is really a rose. Minute red heps follow the flowers. Vigorous to 20ft.

Mme Alfred Carrière: 1897. The loosely cupped double flowers, white with a hint of cream or blush, go well with both old and modern roses, and this climber does well on a north wall. There is a good display in June, spasmodic blooming thereafter, and I have seen flowers on it as late as November. Sweetly scented, it grows to 25ft and has light but rather dull green leaves, which are unusually rounded. A climber that thrives, as they say, on neglect, so forget the pruning.

Meg: 1954. Its very large semi-double flowers are a mixture of

pink and apricot with amber stamens, and they come in June.
There is said to be a second flush later if the heps, which set very
freely, are all removed. Because of the 15ft vigour of the rose and
the lack of it on my part I have never given it a fair test, and I
doubt if many other people have either. Certainly I get no repeat
blooming, but the first flowering is extremely beautiful. Meg has
mildew on occasions but it is easily controllable, and I have never
seen it with black spot. The new canes are dusky red and the
leaves large, dark green and glossy. GM 1954.

Mermaid: 1918. This is a climber about which I have mixed
feelings. It is certainly almost always in flower during the summer
from mid-June onwards, and each individual bloom (they grow
in clusters) is a thing of extreme beauty, but for me there are
rarely enough of them at one time. I feel a climbing rose should
essentially be something for mass effect, as one cannot inspect
individual flowers closely if they are much more than six feet
from the ground. Those of Mermaid are large, single, and sulphur-
yellow, deepening towards the centre, where there are amber
stamens. You buy the plant growing in a pot and very tiny it
seems when it arrives, for it does not take kindly to moving when
it has reached any size. This means, of course, that you must also
wait rather longer than usual for it to achieve its eventual 20 or
30ft, but plenty of space must be allowed for it, for it will become
a real monster, with deadly, hooked prickles. If possible choose a
sheltered wall, for it is not always completely hardy.

Another of Mermaid's quirks is that it does not like pruning
and, as its canes are brittle and snap off easily where they join the
main stems, care is needed in training it. A great advantage is
that its shiny foliage is almost evergreen and seems to be proof
against all disease.

New Dawn, The: 1930. A sport from the once-flowering rambler,
Dr Van Fleet, this, if you please, is a good, repeating climber.
It has a fine second flush in the autumn and some roses in between
as well, but it is not quite so vigorous as the older rose and will
not go much above 10ft, which is quite enough for a number of
situations. The small-to-medium sized, blush-pink blooms are
produced in clusters with great freedom and they are fragrant.

The leaves are dark green and glossy and healthy as a rule, though they can get a touch of mildew. Good as a pillar rose or for a low wall.

Paul's Himalayan Musk Rambler: Definitely only for the big garden, for it will go up a tree to 40ft, from which great sprays will hang down in July of exquisite small, scented, double flowers of blush pink. Do not try to grow it up the flowering cherry on the lawn. It really does need very strong support, or to be allowed to ramble over old and not too precious shrubs in the wild garden if you have got such a thing – intentionally and not by accident. There it will form a vast, impenetrable mound from which one would not be surprised to hear even Sleeping Beauty's Prince calling plaintively to be let out.

Paul's Lemon Pillar: 1915. Very little lemon about this fine old climber as it is, to all intents and purposes, white. If you peer hard you can see a touch of pale yellow at the heart of its huge, very full blooms which, considering the number of petals, do very well in wet weather. It is rather later in coming into flower than the majority of climbers, but from mid-June until well into July it is covered with its exhibition-sized, shapely blooms, which come in clusters of three or four. The petals drop cleanly when the flowers are over and enormous heps are formed, which are not very ornamental and really ought to be removed. It is vigorous up to 10 or 15ft which means that, despite its name, it is not exactly a pillar rose, but care should be taken to train it as horizontally as possible, as it is a rose that rarely sends up new shoots from any-where near the base, so that it can become bare lower down. Growing it up through something like a *chaenomeles*, which will flower earlier and which will have leaves down to ground level, overcomes this problem. The dark green, matt foliage is not proof against mildew and it is likely to need spraying.

Climbing Peace: 1942. In the climate we have in this country, and if you are just married, you will probably have one bloom in time for your silver wedding and maybe a second for your golden wedding. There will be plenty of leaves, though, if that is what you want. Only for hotter countries than ours, though you will find it in some catalogues.

Rambling Rector: A name with a real Victorian flavour about it for a rambler bearing masses of richly fragrant, small, white, semi-double blooms. Reaching 20ft, it is ideal for pergolas or for screening tumbledown sheds and old tree stumps. July flowering.

Ramona: A very distinctive rambler, a sport from R. *anemonoides* which received an AM in 1900. Not unlike those of a clematis, the large single blooms are a particularly lovely blend of crimson lake and pale pink, with a pinkish-grey reverse to the petals. They are scented and appear in early June on a plant that really needs the protection of a sunny wall to give of its best. A real treasure, worth building a wall for.

Seven Sisters: A rambler, introduced from China in 1817, this rose gets its name from the fact that the large clusters of semi-double flowers often have seven different tints, ranging from mauve, through pink, to almost pure white. Not noticeably fragrant. Vigorous to 30ft, flowering in July over a long period.

PLATE 21

Modern Shrub roses   *page*

1. Maigold   130
2. Nymphenburg   130
3. Peace   130
4. Reveil Dijonnais   181
5. Queen Elizabeth   131
6. Uncle Walter   131
7. Scarlet Fire   131
8. Sparrieshoop   131

1	2	3
4	5	6
7		8

Veilchenblau: 1909. At certain stages, probably the nearest to true blue of any rose. Typical rambler heads of small, semi-double flowers, opening a purplish blue, fading to more of a lilac blue, and opening to reveal a white eye and occasional white streaks on the petals. Sweet scent and light, bright green, glossy foliage. A rambler that does not seem to suffer from mildew on a wall, even a north one, but the beholder will suffer from the combination of colours if it is against red brick. July flowering; 15ft.

Wedding Day: A comparatively modern rambler, dating from 1951, but in the old style. It is vigorous to 20ft, with glossy, leathery, mid-green leaves and a tremendous display of bloom in mid-summer. The white, scented flowers open from yellow buds and have pointed petals like little stars. This effect alone makes it worth growing, but it must be said that the blooms fade with a purplish tinge and become spotted and streaked after rain. AM 1950.

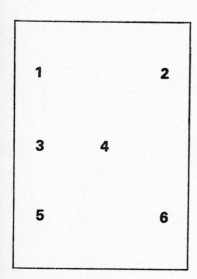

PLATE 22

Modern Shrub roses   *page*

1. Albéric Barbier   134
2. Alister Stella Gray   136
3. *brunonii* La Mortala   136
4. *banksiae lutea*   136
5. Cecile Brunner, climbing   136
6. Félicité et Perpétue   139

Zéphirine Drouhin: An 1868 Bourbon climber that is very robust and hardy, will grow anywhere, is easy to train, and is useful for pillar, fence, pergola, wall or arch, and can be grown as a shrub or used for a hedge if given some support. Growing up to about 15ft, it has light green leaves, coppery when young and not proof against mildew. It needs careful placing in relation to other roses because of the vivid cerise-pink of its loosely double, 3in, fragrant flowers, with which it gives a spectacular display in July, provided that it is reasonably dry. It is supposed to be perpetual, but in my experience the autumn show is pretty sad looking, particularly if you still have the early show in your mind's eye. Oh, and I nearly forgot; it is thornless – or almost completely so.

CHAPTER 17

Increasing Your Stock – Free

Taking Rooted Offsets and Cuttings: Your stock of most shrub roses can quite easily be increased by either of these methods. Offsets from a rose that does not send out suckers can, of course, only be obtained if the parent plant is growing on its own roots, or on a budded bush if it has been planted more deeply than usual, so that the bases of the canes are well below ground level and can form some roots of their own, much as a cutting does. Roses that spread naturally by suckers, like the Scotch Roses, the Gallicas and most of the Rugosas, for instance, and ground coverers, like Max Graf and R. *paulii rosea* which will spread by forming roots where the branches touch the ground, are also ideal for this type of propagation.

To find a suitable rooted top growth from a non-suckering rose, gently scrape away some of the soil round your parent rose in August or September and see if there are any shoots with fine roots growing from their bases, but above the rootstock if there is one. Cut away any suitable cane with a sharp knife, very gently as the hair roots will be very fragile and easily damaged. If on the other hand you are after suckers, you can take these at any time that they appear above the ground, pulling them away from the parent, rather than cutting, but doing this once more very gently to preserve the new roots. Make sure that it is not a sucker from the rootstock unless you know that the rose is on its own roots.

Both kinds of offsets can be planted in a sheltered corner where they can get plenty of light but not the full heat of the midday sun. If a shoot or sucker is very long, it can safely be cut back to about half its length, but try to leave three or four leaves on it. A little peat and sand in the planting hole if the soil is heavy should give it a good start. Keep it watered and it should grow away quite happily, ready for planting out in its final home the following autumn. Finally a warning. Treat your offset like a piece of fine porcelain throughout the planting. Anything more than the gentlest firming in and you may tear the roots right away from it.

Cuttings: Increase of stock by cuttings will take rather longer and there can be no guarantee that all your cuttings will form roots, or survive even if they do start into growth. They have a maddening tendency to collapse suddenly for no apparent reason, even though they may have formed buds and leaves and possibly a flower or two in their first year. Such infant flowers should not be allowed to develop beyond the early bud stage, as all the strength of the developing plant should be diverted underground. Good roots are the most important thing to encourage at this stage.

Despite their unpredictability, a reasonable proportion of the cuttings should form useful plants. Ramblers and most species and near species roses root easily and flourish thereafter, and I have been about seventy-five per cent successful with Bourbons, Gallicas, Rugosa Hybrids, Albas and China Roses. Centifolias there is conflicting evidence about, and I have never tried them myself. It will cost you nothing to try and you could well be

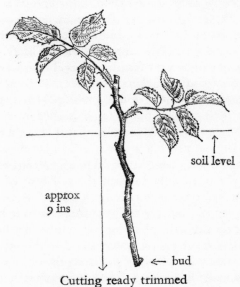

soil level

approx
9 ins

← bud

Cutting ready trimmed

lucky where others have failed. Half the fun of gardening is in experiment and one can never be absolutely sure what is going to happen.

Cuttings can be taken at any time during the months of September, October or November. My own experience is that the earlier two months give the most consistent results as the soil is still warm then. Choose firm, well ripened growth of the current year and shoots that have flowered but on which the flowers are now over. This is not absolutely essential, but it is a good way of knowing that they will be ripe. Cut the shoots into 9in lengths, just above and just below a bud, strip off the thorns and remove the leaves, except for two or three at the top.

Put your cuttings in a bucket of water to keep them fresh and dig a narrow, slit-like trench, 6in deep, in a corner of the garden where a hedge or bushes will keep off the midday sun but where there is still plenty of light. If your soil is heavy, scatter a little sand at the bottom of the trench. In light soil such as I have in my garden, you can simply push your spade 6in into the earth along the line you have chosen and move it backwards and forwards to open out your slit, rather than digging an actual trench.

It will help root formation if you use one of the hormone rooting powders sold by all garden shops. Dip the bottom ends of your cuttings in this one by one as you remove them from the bucket, shake off any surplus powder, and push them down into the slit or trench (about 6in apart) so that the ends with the leaves on are about 3in above ground level. In other words, two-thirds of the cuttings should be in the soil. Two-thirds of their length, that is. Fill in the trench or slit and firm well. Finally a good watering will help things along and keep them watered if the weather is dry.

The cuttings will need no further attention except to tread firmly round them after frosts during the winter which may have loosened them in the soil.

In the spring, most of them should grow away, form shoots and leaves and maybe a flower or two, the latter being removed as before. In the autumn they can be transplanted to their permanent quarters, but I find it better simply to transplant them about 1ft apart in the same sheltered nursery bed and to let them grow on for another year, again removing any flower buds. In this way you can be much more certain just which ones are going to survive and form sturdy plants.

When transplanting rooted cuttings they should be eased apart very gently if the roots of neighbours are intertwined, because they will be just as fragile as those on the offsets I described earlier. You really have to allow three years, except perhaps in the case of the very rampant ramblers, before you can expect to have bushes of a reasonable size.

Pliny, writing in the time of the Romans, said that cuttings should be planted at intervals of one foot when the west wind is blowing. As this latter probably meant that there was rain about, his advice was pretty sound. Things do not change much in the garden.

Budding: Nearly all the roses you buy will be budded on to the tough roots of species or near species. This means that a bud of the kind of rose you have ordered will have been grafted into the neck of the rootstock, just above the roots themselves. This bud will grow into your rose and generally speaking will be tougher, longer-lived, and more vigorous. The top growth of the species is cut completely away in the January or February after budding, leaving only the new shoots of the rose you want. Suckers are, of course, an attempt by the species to restart a life of its own again. No one, admiring a beautiful rose, says: 'Good old rootstock', so you cannot really blame it.

Apart from probably producing more vigorous plants (except for certain species which will be vigorous anyway) you can increase your stock of roses much more quickly by budding than by taking cuttings and, once you have the knack, the percentage of success is much higher, which is why budding is used commercially. The roses which arrive from the nursery will have been budded only the previous year and will, of course, grow into substantial plants and flower well in their first year with you.

You can grow your own rootstocks from scratch if you wish, though if you do this from cuttings taken from wild roses growing in the hedges you will have to add at least another year to your time for the cuttings themselves to grow. It is better to try to get either well rooted offsets from hedge briers, or you may be able to find rooted suckers on your own roses if you have neglected to remove them. It is surprisingly easy, even if you are keeping a regular sucker patrol, to miss the odd one or two until it has grown to quite a respectable size, but all in all it is really best, unless you are only going to bud two or three roses, to buy your rootstocks from your local specialist rose nursery. There are also one or two firms which grow only rootstocks, supplying them to the trade in the main, but which will accept an order for ten or more from individuals.

Whichever source you buy from, describe the type of soil in your garden when you order them and you will get the kind of stock that suits it best. They are not all the same and, while all will grow your roses, some do much better on light soils and some on heavy. Some will give a more vigorous bush, but one that will, perhaps, not live quite so long as one that is budded on a stock that is all for a more compact but longer life. Tell your supplier what your conditions are, and he will give you what you need.

Your local rose nursery is likely to use only one kind, and the chances are that it will be right for you, too. It is worth trying to get the ideal, but it is not a disaster if you are stuck with no choice at all.

When you have got the stocks, they should be planted in November as with any other rose, preferably in a special bed or an odd corner of the vegetable garden or allotment if you have one. They should be about 2½ft apart, and by late June or early in July, budding time, you should have healthy plants. Choose if you can, warm, showery weather in either of these two months. Budding can be done in September as well, but if you leave it till then you will have no chance until the following year to re-bud any stocks that may not have taken. If your first budding is done early you can use a warm September day for this.

For the actual budding, you will need a sharp penknife or preferably a proper budding knife, some raffia, a damp rag, and a bucket of water. A budding knife is not cheap – nearer £2 than £1 – so you may hesitate about getting one if you are only going to do a few roses. It is very like a penknife, but one end is of bone, flattened and pointed, and this is much less likely to tear the bark of the rose than a steel blade. Actually a budding knife does make a very good penknife when not being put to its proper use, but if you are going to combine the two functions, make sure that the steel blade is really sharp when budding time comes round again.

There is, as I mentioned earlier, a knack to successful budding and it may take a little practice to acquire it. If you have not in the past inadvertently left an order of roses on the top of the central heating boiler for a week and then tried to return them to your local rose-grower as being of inferior quality, he is quite likely to let you come and watch his professional budder at work in the nursery and to show you how to do it. There is no doubt at all that this is the best way to learn. Here is the second best.

Cut some sound, well grown shoots of the current year's growth from a bush of the variety that you want to increase. As with taking cuttings, the shoots should have flowered, but the

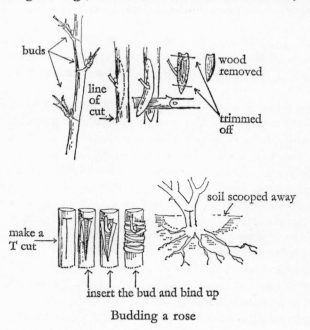

Budding a rose

flowers should be over. You can generally get three to four good buds from the middle portion of a shoot, and as you use one bud per rootstock, simple multiplication (if multiplication can ever be simple) should tell you how many shoots you will need – allowing for making a mess of one or two attempts. Put the shoots in the bucket of water to keep them fresh and scrape away about two to three inches of soil round the neck of the first stock. Wipe it clean with the damp rag and then with the budding (or pen-) knife, cut a T-shaped slit in the bark, just penetrating the bark itself but no more. The downstroke of the T should be about $\frac{3}{4}$in long and the cross stroke, which will run round the neck of the stock, about $\frac{1}{2}$in.

Now take one of your shoots out of the bucket and, with a scooping action, cut out one of the buds. Start your cut about $\frac{1}{2}$in above the bud, passing under it to about one-third of the diameter of the shoot, and coming out again about $\frac{1}{2}$in below it. Trim off the leaf, leaving the leaf stalk, which will now act as a handle to the scion, which is what you now have in your hand.

Now comes the trickiest bit. You will have scooped out a sliver of the wood of the rose underneath the bud, and this must be removed without damaging the underside of the bud itself. Hold the scion between the finger and thumb of one hand, and lever one end of the slip of wood up from the bark with the thumbnail of the other hand. As soon as you have enough of the wood free to get a grip on, give it a quick, sideways twist, when one of several things may happen. You may lose your grip on the scion. You may crush it by holding it too tight. The sliver of wood may come away and most of the bark with it. It may break and only partly come away. It may come right away, taking the underside of the bud with it and leaving a little hollow or depression under the bud. Or – it may come away perfectly, leaving behind it the bark and the little greeny-white, slightly raised base of the bud.

If the latter has happened, you have the knack, and the bud should be put in a safe place, not on the grass, where it will immediately vanish. With the bone point of your budding knife, or the blunt side of your penknife blade, lever up a triangular flap of bark on each side of the T-shaped cut in the stock. Trim

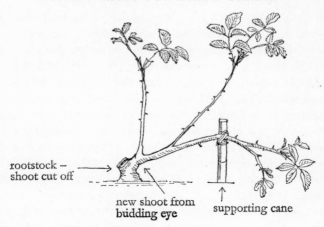

rootstock –
shoot cut off

new shoot from
budding eye

supporting **cane**

Supporting a newly budded shoot

the bark of the scion top and bottom, so that it is about half an inch long altogether and then, holding the scion by the leaf stalk handle, slide it gently but firmly into the T-cut from the top, so that it slips in under the bark of the stock. When it is down as far as it will go, dampen a piece of raffia and bind it round, again gently but firmly, above and below the protruding leaf stalk, leaving only a small gap through which the bud can grow. That is it. You can now move on to the next stock.

If after three weeks the buds remain green and plump, they are likely to have taken. Eventually they will begin to swell and grow, by which time the raffia should have rotted and fallen away. If it has not, remove it carefully. Then leave things alone until the following spring.

When the new shoot has reached perhaps six to nine inches in length it is wise to tie it to a small stake pushed into the ground beside it, to prevent it being too boisterously blown about by the wind and possibly wrenched away from its still-forming union with the stock. At the same time all the top growth of the stock should be cut away just above the union. In the autumn, your new roses can be transplanted to their final home.

Hybridising: The processes so far described will increase the numbers of roses that you already have, or let you add to your range of known varieties if you have been given (or you have stolen) the cuttings from a friend's garden, or have smuggled them into the country in a sponge-bag at the end of your holiday.

Hybridising will produce for you a completely new rose, exclusively your own.

Most professional hybridisers in recent years have concentrated on crossing Hybrid Teas and floribundas. Little has been done with species or the old roses except by a very few breeders, such as Wilhelm Kordes in Germany, who has been using species successfully to increase the hardiness of roses in a country where they can be subjected to great extremes of heat and cold. His work has produced a remarkable range of very tough and hardy climbers and shrubs, including Frühlingsgold and its cousins through crossings with the Scotch Roses, and he has further developed the Hybrid Musks with varieties like Wilhelm and Hamburg. More recently, Samuel McGredy in Ireland has used Frühlingsmorgen in his breeding programme to produce the multi-coloured floribunda Picasso, and Edward Le Grice in England has made use of the Gallica, Tuscany, as a parent for his magenta floribunda, News. That wonderful and comparatively modern shrub rose, Nevada, has R. *moyesii* as one of its parents (though do not try breeding from Nevada, which is sterile).

There are others, including roses like Constance Spry, bred to resemble the old roses and resulting from a cross between the Gallica, Belle Isis, and the floribunda, Dainty Maid, but these samples are the exceptions and the ground has scarcely been touched. Roses that have lived for hundreds of years must have something worthwhile to hand on, so why not try crossing some of your old ones, either amongst each other, or with modern varieties as the fancy takes you? Admittedly the chances of producing something that is really first-rate, let alone sensationally new is about one in 20,000. You will not be able to borrow money on your prospects of making a fortune out of breeding, but you will have a lot of fun. Cross two roses and you may get almost anything as a result except a chrysanthemum.

It is easier to control temperature, humidity, insect interference and so on if you hybridise in a greenhouse, growing the roses in pots. It is not, however, so easy to control a 10ft by 10ft shrub rose, or rather two of them, mother and father, in the same confines. So, if you want to do it under glass, use naturally small varieties or catch them young. More probably you will want to work from bushes already established in your garden, which is perfectly possible, though the seed pods are that bit less likely to ripen properly and accidental pollination by insects must be particularly guarded against.

Just when you carry out your crosses will depend to some extent on the flowering time of your two parent roses. Late June is the ideal time for most, but not if you want to cross something with, say, Canarybird, which would be over by then, or with R. *wichuraiana* or its offspring, ramblers which might not have started to flower. But remember one thing; the later you do it, the less time there is for the heps to ripen.

The roses that are to be the seed parent (the one that will form the heps and hence the seeds) and the pollen parent should both be at the loose bud stage, about one-third open, but not enough to show the stamens which might allow insects to get at them before you do. With some of the single and fast-opening species, the right timing is especially important.

Taking the seed parent first, very gently peel away all the petals

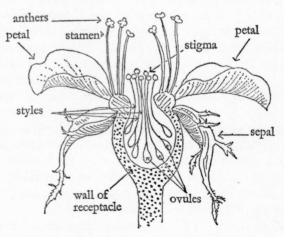

Section through a rose flower

of the flower you have chosen, taking care to leave no pieces behind which might in due course set up rot in the hep. Using nail scissors, snip off the stamens or anthers, leaving the stigma exposed, and then put a small polythene bag over the whole thing, loosely tied so that it will not blow away. This will keep the insects away until the actual pollination is carried out on the following day.

Take the pollen parent next and fold back the petals gently and remove the stamens with a pair of tweezers, putting them into a clean dish or saucer. Store it in a safe place overnight.

By the following day both parents of the cross should be ready. The stamens of the pollen parent will have dried out and shed some of their pollen into the saucer, and the stigma of the seed parent will be glistening and sticky, so that the yellow grains of pollen will adhere to it.

Either with your finger or with a clean water-colour brush, brush some of the pollen on to the stigma of the seed parent and the cross is made. If you are using a brush and doing several different crosses, make sure that it is absolutely clean between each cross or you may get the wrong pollen on the wrong flower.

An alternative method of crossing is to prepare the seed parent as before, but to pick the whole flower head of the pollen parent. For the actual cross, fold back the petals of the pollen parent and brush its anthers on to the stigma of the other, transferring the pollen that way. Finally, for either method, replace the polythene bag over the seed parent and label it with a weather-proof label showing what rose you have crossed with it. Do not imagine that you will remember, particularly if you have done several different crossings, because I can assure you from experience that you will not.

The bag can be removed after about five days as the seed should by then be set and will rebuff the approaches of the most seductive of insects.

During the months that follow, the heps you have pollinated should begin to swell. If they do, all the signs are that you have been successful and the cross has taken. In late November they can be cut from the bush and buried, stalk upwards, in damp sand or peat in flowerpots, not forgetting to transfer the labels to the pots as well. Leave them out of doors in a place that will be exposed to any weather that is going, including frost, but safe from raiding fieldmice.

In January, remove the heps from the sand and separate the seeds from the soft, rotten flesh of the heps. Do this, one hep at a time, keeping the appropriate label nearby, or you will get the heps and the seeds inextricably mixed. Float the seeds, which are quite large and easily handled individually, in a saucer of water. Those that sink to the bottom are the ones that should grow.

The seeds should be planted one at a time about 1½in apart and one-third of an inch deep in a seed tray containing John Innes or other similar seed compost, and with a little sand sprinkled over the top to prevent moss forming. The trays can be left out of doors or kept in an unheated greenhouse.

As a matter of fact the seeds can also be planted straight into the ground, though the rate of loss may be fairly high from one reason or another, including the aforementioned outlaw bands of fieldmice. If you do this, choose a spot which will not get the midday sun should there happen to be any during the coming summer.

Some of the seeds will come up that year, some not till the following year, and some not at all. You cannot hurry the germination of rose seeds. And do not expect too much of the first rather pathetic flowers you will get. These are likely to be a shock to you, washed-out looking and probably single, even from double parents, but those of the following year should give you more of an idea of what you have really got. The new plants will probably mildew badly, so this should be guarded against and the really bad ones discarded, however heartbreaking this may be. Anything that shows promise in the second year should be budded on to a rootstock to develop its true potential.

CHAPTER 18

Seeing Them for Yourself

THE fact that you should see what you are going to buy before you buy it is not peculiar to roses. It is common sense, but it is not quite so easy with plants as it is with most other things because, when you buy, you do not usually buy the finished product. Even if you go and look at roses growing in a nursery, you will be seeing one-year-old bushes which will not have reached anything like their full size and final form. This is particularly so with shrub roses, which mostly grow much bigger than other kinds. You can get some idea of what they will be like, certainly, and you can get a very good idea if the nursery happens to have display beds or show gardens where the roses grow permanently as examples of the varieties they stock. Unfortunately, however, nurseries with really good display beds of shrub roses are not very common.

You can see a few varieties in parks, but as often as not they will not be labelled and there will be no one to ask. So you may have to go farther afield.

Many of the National Trust gardens and the gardens of other big country houses open to the public have magnificent collections, where you can see not only the roses in their full glory, but can also pick up no end of tips on how to use them to the best advantage. Nymans in Sussex, Sissinghurst Castle in Kent, Tintinhull in Somerset, Bodnant in Denbighshire in Wales, Wallington in Northumberland, Hardwick Hall in Derbyshire and Rowallane and Mount Stewart – on the shores of Strangford Lough – in Northern Ireland are notable examples. Brayfordbury, which contains the National Rose Species Collection, is in Hertfordshire, only twenty-five miles from London. Here real rose history is shown, but it is a working garden and only open one day in the year under the National Gardens Scheme. Kew Gardens, the Savill and Valley Gardens at Windsor, the Royal

Horticultural Society's gardens at Wisley in Surrey, also have good collections, as does Queen Mary's Rose Garden in Regent's Park and the display garden at the headquarters of the Royal National Rose Society at Chiswell Green, near St Albans. Mottisfont Abbey, in Hampshire, is busy establishing a national collection. There are many others of course, but the few I have mentioned will, I hope, give a lead in different parts of the country. It is best to see as wide a range of roses as you can before making your final choice or you may miss some beauties. A book like this can, I hope, be a useful guide and tell you quite a lot about how to look after them when you have got them, but no book can, for instance, give a real picture of the final size and *mass* of a shrub. This last is most important when planning a shrub garden, particularly with the larger varieties. Dimensions are of some help, but only as a rough indication.

And once you have seen the roses and made your choice, how do you get them?

As I have said earlier, you will not at present find shrub roses

PLATE 23

Climbing and Rambling roses   page

in pre-packed form in stores and supermarkets, and if they do eventually come, it is likely to be a long time before any worth-while range is available. It is not the best way in any case to buy roses, as they are often kept for long periods in unsuitable conditions.

Many small local nurseries and garden centres, too, do not stock them, or at most have only one or two of the best-known varieties, like Nevada and Canarybird and perhaps one or two of the Rugosas. It is tempting to buy these just because they are there, but not very wise unless what the nursery has got is what you were looking for anyway. If you have planned carefully, and get a rose that you did not intend to buy, you may end up with something that just does not fit your scheme.

Fortunately, more and more nurseries are beginning to increase their range, or to stock shrub roses where they did not before, but it is best, and really very little trouble, to send for a catalogue from one of the specialist growers or one of the more general rose nurseries that already carry a large assortment and order

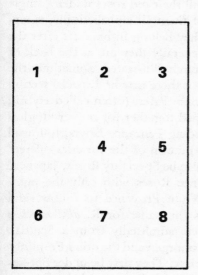

from that. In this way you will get what you want, get good plants into the bargain – and you will only have to worry about the spelling of the names and not the pronunciation.

Among the firms that could be of interest are Cockers of Aberdeen, Harkness of Hitchin, Gandy's Roses, Cants of Colchester, John Mattock near Oxford, Le Grice in Norfolk, Waterers, John Scott in Somerset, Jackmans of Woking, in Surrey, and the real specialists like Sunningdale Nurseries, Murrell's of Shrewsbury and Hillier's of Winchester, the latter more particularly for species. Also Albrighton Roses of Wolverhampton.

Most of these will have catalogues in which the roses are classified in much the same way as the lists in this book. Between them, they will cover all the roses that I mention, and some of them will have many others, but only one of the real specialists is likely to be a single source for my complete range. I have tried, however, to pick varieties which are good and also not too difficult to find.

A number of nurseries group all their old roses under a single heading of Shrub Roses, and list them all alphabetically, sometimes with the group to which they belong in brackets after the variety name, sometimes not. Generally they are at the back of the catalogue and unfortunately rarely illustrated. Sometimes the heading is Old Fashioned Roses, or there may be a special section for Hybrid Musk Roses or Penzance Briers (often called Hybrid Sweet Briers), with the rest lumped together for no very logical reason. I have even seen the heading Penzance Briers, followed by the price per bush, but no indication of the varieties offered.

Other variations on the theme can be Speciality Roses, Japanese Roses to cover Rugosas, Provence Roses with only the uninformative Red Provence and White Provence to follow, and Bonnie Prince Charlie's Rose as the name for R. *alba maxima* (The Jacobite Rose), the last one admittedly from a Scottish nursery. Frühlingsgold, Frühlingsmorgen and the other Frühlings roses tend to end up all over the place. They may be under Species Roses, Scotch Roses, or Modern Shrub Roses, and the Rugosa hybrids are often listed as species. The shrub-type floribundas and Hybrid Teas can be amongst the modern shrubs or with the others of their kind, and Hybrid Perpetuals are often with the Hybrid Teas.

All of which is not meant as a discouragement. It is simply an indication that you may not find the rose you are looking for exactly where you expect it. But keep looking. It is often not the nursery's fault. I have already explained how even the greatest of experts can differ.

Except for those from the specialists, catalogues are not usually very informative about their shrub roses, though they are getting better. In catalogue language, Medium Sized means small, Moderate Growth means weakly, Vigorous means normal growth and Does Well Under Glass means a rose is quite hopeless in the rain, but perhaps most of this applies more to Hybrid Teas and floribundas than to shrub roses. There was a refreshing frankness about an advertisement for Hobbies Ltd roses towards the end of the last century when they said: "Write to us for quotations and see our Catalogue, which we will send post free for the actual cost of the postage – 3d."

One important point. Order early. Stocks of some shrub roses will not be large, though they should be slowly building up as demand increases. Do not be tempted by the offers of cheap hedging roses that you see in the press. They are often simply poor quality briers and a waste of money.

And now for a change of subject. If you want to learn more about shrub roses and to become a real expert, growing them yourself is the best way. But here is a little about a number of books that will help you to go deeper than I have done in mine. Most general rose books contain at least a small section on the subject, but for really comprehensive and scholarly advice and fascinating history, Graham Thomas's two books, *The Old Shrub Roses* and *Shrub Roses of Today*, cannot be beaten. His *Climbing Roses Old and New* is also the most authoritative work on the subject. The Annual of the Royal National Rose Society (free to members) features many articles on the old roses and, among other modern books – though expensive – Nancy Steen's *The Charm of Old Roses* (she grows hers in New Zealand, but much of the information is just as applicable here), and S. M. Gault and Patrick Synge's *The Dictionary of Roses in Colour* give between them about the best range of colour photographs of the old roses that you could find.

There are a number of older books, too, many of them written in Victorian times, when the roses they describe were at the height of their popularity. They can still be obtained second-hand, though again, many of them will be expensive as they are now collector's items. Gertrude Jekyll and Edward Mawley's *Roses for English Gardens* is one that is particularly good on the uses to which the various old roses can be put. It also, believe it or not, contains a chapter on Roses in English Gardens on the Riviera. How times change.

S. Reynolds Hole's (Dean Hole) *A Book About Roses* (he was a founder of the RNRS) is one of the best written, amusing and instructive books on the subject ever. Three other Victorian clergymen, the Rev. H. D'Ombrian with his *Roses for Amateurs*, the Rev. Joseph Pemberton (who created the Hybrid Musks), and the Rev. Foster Melliar with his *The Book of the Rose*, produced works that have become classics in their field. The latter is a pretty serious book, much concerned with growing roses for exhibition, but contains at least one nice story.

"On one occasion," he writes, "when dining at a friend's home, I had some plum-pudding handed me, of the modern type, very dark, rich, strong and greasy. I declined it, but regarded it curiously and with interest, my thoughts wandering elsewhere. My hostess, noticing my earnest gaze, asked me if I saw anything the matter with it. Without thinking, and naturally with somewhat unfortunate results, I blurted out the truth: 'Oh, no: I was thinking what rare stuff it would be to grow roses in!' "

Two eminent nurserymen of the time also produced works that have lasted and deservedly so. Thomas Rivers wrote his *The Rose Amateur's Guide*, and if you are prepared to go up to about £25 for a good first edition (there are later editions without the colour plates which are cheaper), there is William Paul's *The Rose Garden*. Paul (of Paul's Scarlet and Paul's Lemon Pillar) was probably the leading English rose nurseryman of his day. His book, a standard work in his time, contains some charming wood engravings in addition to the colour plates, covers every conceivable aspect of rose history and culture, and has long lists of

varieties which were then popular and comments on their performance. The historical side is of great interest, though recent
research has shown that some of the theories that Paul advances
will no longer hold water. Rose culture, too, has progressed, and
we do not now have to carry out the following procedure when
dealing with greenfly: "– syringing with tobacco water or dusting
with snuff and soot when the leaves are damp, that the mixture
may adhere thereto, destroys or disperses it. It is also good
practice to smoke the trees with tobacco, using the fumigating-
bellows, first enclosing the head with some material that will
prevent the escape of the smoke." It is interesting, too, that Paul
classes roses that flower in late summer, and remember that they
were comparatively new at that time, as Autumnal Roses and
mentions that some people recommend the cutting off of the
early summer flush of buds to give a better show later on. He
does not, however, endorse the idea himself.

Rather more recent, though now out of print and again in the
collector's class and very scarce are Edward Bunyard's *Old
Garden Roses* and Sitwell and Russell's *Old Garden Roses* in two
volumes, each with eight superb colour plates.

Ellen Wilmot's *The Genus Rosa*, and even more so Redouté's
Les Roses, are not only strictly for collectors, but for collectors
who are also millionaires. There are, however, two very well
printed selections from Redouté's plates published by The Ariel
Press under the titles Roses (A Selection) and Roses 2 (A Selection).
Care is needed here, though, as the classification of many of the
roses has been altered and the names on many of the plates may
be misleading. For instance, Empress Josephine, which we also
know as R. *francofurtana*, is listed firstly as R. *turbinata*. A much
fuller list of useful books can be found in the bibliography.

Well, we are nearly at the end. Almost all books about old
roses begin with the author reminiscing about the roses of his
childhood. This one is different. It is going to end with them,
though the reminiscences may be a little different, too.

Although my mother was a keen gardener and lover of roses,
I cannot remember a single one from my early days. I cannot
remember gleaming silver bowls of Mrs John Laing or Maréchal
Niel on the hall table as we set out for church on Sundays. I

cannot remember the chamois blooms of Gloire de Dijon or the pink ones of Mme Gregoire Staechelin round the cottage door. I date from the Hybrid Musk era, anyway. Vanity and I are the same age, though not otherwise similar. The first rose bush I remember I fell into off a wall. I could describe the prickles, but not the flowers.

Finally I would claim a record. This is the first book ever written on old roses in which they have not been described as The Queen of Flowers. Be thankful for that, if for nothing else.

Summary Chart of Roses Described

This chart attempts the almost impossible task of summarising a large part of what I have said in the chapters of this book that describe the varieties and species in detail. I think that it may prove useful as a quick guide, particularly if you have very definite requirements on basic points like the usual approximate size, continuity of flowering, and so on. Otherwise, tread carefully.

How, for instance, can you summarise the colour of a rose that may blend through many tones, from the palest pink on the outer petals, to Rupert Brooke's "Red darkness of the heart of roses"? Pink/Red hardly has the same ring about it.

And again with habit. A shrub rose may not become as bushy as it should if it is grown in the wrong place, is starved, or is simply a bad plant of that particular variety to start with. It will also not be as large. Flowering periods may differ slightly according to climate, and scent varies with temperature, time of year, and also for no discernible reason. The scent scale in the chart reflects what I have found myself; that is all I can say. Only the other day a friend said to me that one of the reasons he did not like Iceberg was that it was scentless. I like it and find it has a delicate but marked perfume. Which, I realise, is a great help to everyone.

So, all-in-all, use the chart for a first quick assessment, and then look up what you have chosen in the appropriate chapter for the finer points.

Key to abbreviations used in Summary Chart

Type of Flowers	Habit	Uses	Foliage
S = single	B = bushy	Sh = shrub	F = outstanding foliage
S-D = semi-double	O = open	C = climber	Sc = scented
D = double	Sp = spreading	Be = bedding	A = autumn colour
		H = hedge	E = almost evergreen
		P = pillar	

Group/Variety	Flowers					Habit	Uses	Foliage	G... he...
	Colour	Type	Scent	Flowering period	Size				
SPECIES									
Canarybird	yellow	S	4	May	7′×7′	O	Sh	F	–
Cantabrigiensis	cream	S-D	3	May/June	7′×7′	B	Sh	F	
Complicata	pink, white	S	2	June/July	5′×8′	B	Sh C	—	y
Dupontii	pink, cream	S	4	June/July	7′×7′	B	Sh C	—	y
Ecae	yellow	S	2	May/June	5′×4′	O	Sh	F	–
Foetida bicolor	red, yellow	S	4	June/July	5′×4′	O	Sh	—	–
Foetida persiana	yellow	D	4	June/July	5′×4′	O	Sh	—	–
Forrestiana	pink, white	S	3	June/July	7′×7′	O	Sh	—	y
Headleyensis	cream	S	5	May/June	9′×12′	B	Sh	F	y
Macrantha	blush	S	4	June/July	5′×10′	B	Sh	—	y
Macrantha Lady Curzon	pink	S	4	June/July	8′×8′	B	Sh C	—	y
Moyesii	crimson	S	o	May/June	12′×10′	O	Sh	F	y
M. Eos	coral-red	S-D	o	May/June	12′×7′	O	Sh	F	y
M. Geranium	red	S	o	May/June	10′×8′	O	Sh	F	y
M. Highdownensis	pink	S	o	June/July	10′×10′	B	Sh	F	y
M. Nevada	cream	S-D	I	recurrent	7′×7′	B	Sh	—	–
M. Marguerite Hilling	pink	S-D	I	recurrent	7′×7′	B	Sh	—	–
Multibracteata	rose, lilac	S	3	July/Aug	7′×6′	B	Sh	Sc	y
Paulii rosea	pink	S	4	June/July	3′×10′	Sp	Sh	—	–
Pomifera duplex	pink	S-D	2	May/June	7′×7′	B	Sh	—	y
Rubiginosa	pink	S	5	June	8′×8′	O	Sh H	Sc A	y
R. Amy Robsart	pink	S-D	5	June	8′×8′	O	Sh H	Sc A	y
R. Meg Merrilees	crimson	S	5	June	8′×8′	O	Sh H	Sc A	y
R. Lady Penzance	copper	S	5	June	6′×6′	O	Sh H	Sc A	y
R. Lord Penzance	fawn	S	5	June	6′×6′	O	Sh H	Sc A	y
Rubrifolia	pink	S	o	June	6′×6′	O	Sh	F	y
Sericea pteracantha	white	S*	I	May	10′×10′	B	Sh	†	
Soulieana	white	S	4	June/July	10′×10′	B	Sh	F	
Spinosissima Ormiston Roy	yellow	S	3	May/June	4′×4′	B	Sh	—	
S. Frühlingsanfang	ivory	S	5	June	8′×8′	O	Sh	A	
S. Frühlingsgold	yellow	S-D	5	June	9′×9′	O	Sh	—	
S. Frühlingsmorgen	pink, yellow	S	5	recurrent	6′×6′	O	Sh	—	
S. Frühlingsduft	apricot	D	5	June	6′×6′	O	Sh	—	
S. Stanwell Perpetual	white	D	5	recurrent	6′×4′	O	Sh	—	

* Four petals   †Translucent red thorns

p/Variety	Colour	Type	Scent	Flowering period	Size	Habit	Uses	Foliage	Good heps
biana	pink	S	3	May	6'×6'	O	Sh	F	yes
LICAS									
n Blanchard	crimson	S-D	4	June/July	5'×3'	O	Sh	—	yes
e de Crécy	purple, pink	D	5	June/July	4'×3'	O	Sh	—	yes
aieux	pink, splashed purple	D	4	June/July	4'×2'	O	Sh	—	—
linal de Richelieu	maroon	D	5	June/July	5'×3'	B	Sh	—	—
les de Mills	crimson	D	4	June/July	4'×4'	B	Sh	—	—
ress Josephine	purple, pink	D	1	June/July	4'×3'	B	Sh	—	—
y Duval	cherry, crimson	D	4	June/July	4'×3'	B	Sh	—	—
cinalis	crimson	S-D	0	June/July	4'×4'	B	Sh	—	yes
a Mundi	pink, striped white	D	0	June/July	4'×4'	B	Sh H	—	—
asse Tout	cerise-pink	D	4	June/July	4'×4'	B	Sh	—	—
olore de Flandre	white, splashed purple	D	4	June/July	3'×3'	B	Sh	—	—
cany Superb	dark crimson	D	2	June/July	4'×2'	B	Sh	—	—
ASKS									
h Damask	lilac pink	D	5	June	5'×6'	B	Sh	—	—
iana	pink	S-D	5	June/July	5'×4'	B	Sh	—	—
e Hardy	white, green eye	D	5	June/July	6'×5'	O	Sh	—	—
tre Saisons	pink	D	5	perpetual	4'×3'	B	Sh	—	—
Nicholas	pink	S-D	2	June/July	4'×4'	B	Sh	—	yes
k & Lancaster	pink and white	D	4	June/July	6'×6'	B	Sh	—	—
AS									
a maxima	white	D	4	June/July	7'×8'	B	Sh	F	yes
a semi-plena	white	S-D	4	June/July	8'×8'	B	Sh	F	yes
e Amour	pink	S-D	5	June/July	6'×4'	B	Sh	F	yes
stial (Céleste)	pink	S-D	4	June/July	6'×7'	B	Sh	F	—
cité Parmentier	creamy pink	D	5	June/July	4'×3'	B	Sh	F	—
at Maiden's Blush	blush	D	5	June/July	6'×5'	B	Sh	F	—
nigin von anemarck	pink	D	4	June/July	5'×4'	O	Sh	F	—
e Plantier	white	D	4	June/July	5'×6'	B	Sh C H	—	—
den's Blush	blush	D	4	June/July	5'×4'	B	Sh	F	—
TIFOLIAS									
ifolia	pink	D	5	June/July	5'×4'	O	Sh	F	—
peau de Napoleon	pink	D	3	June/July	5'×4'	O	Sh	F	—
Meaux	pink	D	5	June/July	3½'×3'	B	Sh	—	—

Group/Variety	Colour	Type	Scent	Flowering period	Size	Habit	Uses	Foliage
Fantin Latour	pink	D	3	June/July	6'×6'	O	Sh P	—
Petite de Hollande	pink	D	5	June/July	3'×2'	O	Sh	F
Robert le Diable	purple	D	4	June/July	4'×3'	O	Sh	F
Tour de Malakoff	carmine	D	3	June/July	6'×4'	O	Sh P	F
MOSS ROSES								
Capitaine John Ingram	purple	D	4	June/July	5'×4'	B	Sh	F*
Duchesse de Verneuil	pink	D	5	June/July	5'×4'	B	Sh	—
Général Kléber	blush pink	D	5	June/July	5'×4'	B	Sh	F
Gloire de Mousseux	pink	D	4	June/July	4'×4'	B	Sh	—
Henri Martin	crimson	D	4	June/July	5'×4'	B	Sh	—†
Mousseline	pink	D	5	recurrent	4'×4'	B	Sh	—
Nuits de Young	maroon	D	5	June/July	4'×3'	O	Sh	F
William Lobb	purple, fading lilac	D	5	June/July	6'×5'	O	Sh C	—
CHINA & PORTLAND ROSES								
Bloomfield Abundance	pink	D	2	perpetual	6'×7'	O	Sh	F
Cécile Brunner	pink	D	2	perpetual	4'×3'	O	Sh Be	F
Little White Pet	white	D	2	perpetual	2'×2'	O	Sh Be	—
Natalie Nypels	pink	S-D	4	perpetual	2'×2'	B	Sh Be	F
Perle d'Or	cream	D	2	perpetual	4'×3'	O	Sh	—
Serratipetala	crimson	D	1	perpetual	5'×5'	O	Sh	—
Slater's Crimson China‡	crimson	D	4	perpetual	4'×5'	O	Sh	—
Viridiflora	green	D	0	perpetual	4'×3'	O	Sh	—
Comte de Chambord	pink	D	4	perpetual	4'×3'	B	Sh Be	—
Jacques Cartier	pink	D	3	perpetual	4'×3'	B	Sh Be	—
BOURBONS & HYBRID PERPETUALS								
Adam Messerich (B)	pink	S-D	4	recurrent	6'×4'	B	Sh P	—
Boule de Neige (B)	cream, pink	D	5	perpetual	5'×3'	O	Sh	—
Commandant Beaurepaire (B)	pink, striped maroon	D	2	June/July	6'×5'	B	Sh P	—
Ferdinand Pichard (B)	white, striped crimson	D	4	perpetual	4'×4'	O	Sh	—
Frau Karl Druschki (HP)	white	D	0	recurrent	6'×3'	O	Sh Be	—
Général Jacqueminot (HP)	scarlet-crimson	D	4	recurrent	4'×3'	O	Sh Be	—
George Arends (HP)	pink	D	4	recurrent	6'×3'	O	Sh P Be	—
George Dickson (HP)	crimson-purple	D	3	recurrent	5'×3'	O	Sh P Be	—
Honorine de Brabant	lilac, striped crimson	D	4	recurrent	6'×6'	B	Sh P	—

*Red moss   †Scanty moss   ‡Tender

b/Variety	Colour	Type	Scent	Flowering period	Size	Habit	Uses	Foliage	Good heps
		Flowers							
n Dickson (HP)	crimson, scarlet	D	3	recurrent	9′×4′	O	Sh P Be	—	—
leen Harrop (B)	pink	D	3	recurrent	7′×5′	B	Sh C	—	—
eine Victoria (B)	pink	D	4	perpetual	5′×3′	O	Sh	—	—
se Odier (B)	lilac pink	D	4	perpetual	6′×4′	O	Sh	—	—
Ernst Calvat (B)	peach pink	D	5	recurrent	7′×5′	O	Sh P	—	—
Isaac Pereire (B)	carmine	D	5	recurrent	8′×6′	O	Sh P	—	—
Pierre Oger (B)	blush cream	D	4	perpetual	6′×3′	O	Sh	—	—
John Laing (HP)	pink	D	5	recurrent	5′×3′	B	Sh Be	—	—
e Camille de han (HP)	dark crimson	D	4	June/July	4′×3′	O	Sh Be	—	—
e des Violettes (HP)	purple	D	5	perpetual	6′×5′	B	Sh	—	—
r Lambelin (HP)	maroon edged white	D	4	recurrent	4′×3′	O	Sh	—	—
enir de la almaison (B)	blush pink	D	5	perpetual*	5′×4′	B	Sh	—	—
h Brunner (HP)	carmine	D	5	recurrent	6′×4′	O	Sh P Be	—	—
gata di Bologna	lilac, striped crimson	D	3	recurrent	6′×5′	O	Sh P	—	—
uner Knabe (B)	crimson-purple	D	1	June/July	5′×6′	O	Sh	—	yes

OSAS

s	pale amber	D	4	perpetual	7′×5′	B	Sh	F A	—
	white	S	5	perpetual	6′×6′	B	Sh H	F A	yes
Pointevine	pink	S-D	2	perpetual	5′×5′	B	Sh H	F A	†
c Double de ubert	white	S-D	5	perpetual	6′×5′	B	Sh H	F A	—
ad F. Meyer	silver pink	D	4	recurrent	10′×6′	O	Sh P H	—	—
riata	pink	S-D	3	perpetual	5′×4′	B	Sh H	F A	—
Grootendorst	crimson	D	0	perpetual	8′×6′	O	Sh H	F A	—
Dagmar Hastrup	pink	S	5	perpetual	5′×4′	B	Sh H	F A	yes
Graf	pink	S	4	June/July		B	‡	F	—
a Zembla	white	D	4	recurrent	8′×5′	O	Sh P H	—	—
Grootendorst	pink	D	0	perpetual	6′×5′	O	Sh H	F A	—
raie de l'Hay	wine red	S-D	5	perpetual	8′×8′	B	Sh H	F A	—
a van Fleet	rose pink	S-D	4	perpetual	6′×5′	B	Sh P H	—	—
osa	pink	S	4	perpetual	4′×5′	B	Sh H	F A	yes
eezwerg	white	S-D	2	perpetual	4′×5′	B	Sh H	—	yes

RID MUSKS

Beauty	buff, cream	D	4	perpetual	6′×7′	B	Sh P H	—	—
elia	pink, yellow	D	3	perpetual	6′×7′	B	Sh H	—	—
e	apricot	S-D	3	perpetual	4′×3′	B	Sh Be	—	—
ia	pink	D	5	perpetual	5′×6′	B	Sh H Be	—	—

predictable   †Scant heps   ‡Ground cover

Group/Variety	Colour	Flowers Type	Scent	Flowering period	Size	Habit	Uses	Foliage
Francesca	apricot	D	4	perpetual	6′×6′	B	Sh H Be	—
Hamburg	crimson-scarlet	S-D	1	perpetual	6′×4′	O	Sh H	—
Magenta	mauve	D	4	perpetual	4′×4′	O	Sh	
Moonlight	ivory	S-D	4	perpetual	6′×5′	O	Sh P	—
Pax	white	S-D	4	perpetual	6′×6′	B	Sh H	—
Penelope	cream, pink	S-D	5	perpetual	6′×5′	B	Sh H Be	—
Pink Prosperity	pink	D	5	perpetual	5′×4′	B	Sh H Be	—
Prosperity	blush	D	5	perpetual	7′×5′	B	Sh H Be	—
Thisbe	buff	S-D	5	perpetual	4′×4′	B	Sh H Be	—
Vanity	pink	S	5	perpetual	9′×6′	B	Sh H	—
Wilhelm	crimson	S-D	1	perpetual	7′×5′	O	Sh P	—
Will Scarlet	scarlet	S-D	2	perpetual	7′×5′	O	Sh P	—
MODERN SHRUBS								
Aloha	pink	D	5	perpetual	6′×4′	B	Sh P	F
Ballerina	pink, white eye	S	2	recurrent	5′×6′	B	Sh	—
Berlin	scarlet	S	2	recurrent	4′×3′	O	Sh H Be	—
Bonn	salmon, scarlet	D	3	perpetual	6′×4′	O	Sh H	—
Chinatown	yellow	D	4	recurrent	5′×4′	B	Sh H	F
Clair Matin	pink	S-D	2	recurrent	5′×7′	B	Sh H	
Constance Spry	pink	D	4	June/July	7′×7′	B	Sh P	F
Dorothy Wheatcroft	scarlet	S-D	0	recurrent	5′×3′	O	Sh	—
Dortmund	crimson, white eye	S	0	recurrent	5′×8′	O	Sh P	—
Elmshorn	carmine	D	0	recurrent	6′×6′	O	Sh P	—
Erfurt	pink	S-D	3	perpetual	5′×6′	B	Sh	F
First Choice	orange, scarlet	S	2	perpetual	5′×4′	O	Sh Be	—
Fred Loads	vermilion	S	4	perpetual	7′×4′	O	Sh	—
Frensham	scarlet-crimson	S	0	perpetual	4′×4′	B	Sh H Be	F
Fritz Nobis	salmon, pink	S-D	4	June/July	6′×6′	B	Sh	F
Goldbush	peach	S-D	4	June/July	5′×6′	B	Sh P	—
Golden Chersonese	yellow	S	4	May/June	6′×7′	O	Sh	F
Golden Moss	pale yellow	D	3	recurrent	4′×4′	O	Sh	—
Golden Wings	yellow	S	4	perpetual	5′×5′	O	Sh H	—
Gruss an Aachen	flesh pink	D	2	perpetual	2½′×2½′	B	Sh Be	—
Heidelberg	crimson, scarlet	S-D	2	perpetual	6′×4′	O	Sh P	—
Hunter	crimson	D	0	perpetual	6′×5′	B	Sh H	—
Iceberg	white	S-D	3	perpetual	6′×4′	O	Sh Be	—
Joseph's Coat	cherry red	S-D	1	recurrent	6′×8′	O	Sh P H	—
Kassel	carmine	S-D	2	perpetual	7′×6′	O	Sh P H	—
Laughter	salmon	S-D	3	recurrent	6′×4′	O	Sh H	—
Lavender Lassie	pink	D	4	recurrent	5′×4′	O	Sh	F

SUMMARY CHART OF ROSES DESCRIBED

up/Variety	Flowers			Flowering period	Size	Habit	Uses	Foliage	Good heps
	Colour	Type	Scent						
gold	buff yellow	S-D	5	May/June	7'×8'	O	Sh C	—	—
nphenburg	salmon	D	5	recurrent	6'×6'	O	Sh C	—	—
ce	pale yellow	D	1	recurrent	6'×4'	O	Sh Be	F	—
lsen's Park Rose	pink	S-D	3	recurrent	5'×5'	B	Sh H	—	—
en Elizabeth	pink	D	2	perpetual	9'×3'	O	Sh H	—	—
rlet Fire	scarlet	S	o	July	7'×7'	O	Sh P	—	yes
rrieshoop	salmon	S	4	perpetual	6'×4'	O	Sh	—	—
le Walter	crimson, scarlet	D	2	recurrent	5'×3'	O	Sh	—	—
MBERS & RAMBLERS									
ée Vibert	white	D	4	June/July	15'	O	C	—	—
ter Stella Gray	cream	D	4	recurrent	15'	O	C	—	—
éric Barbier	cream	D	3	June/July	15'	O	C	F	—
ertine	pink	D	5	June/July	15'	O	Sh C	—	—
ksiae lutea*	yellow	D	3	May/June	25'	O	C	E	—
onii La Mortala*	cream, white	S-D	5	July/Aug	25'	O	C	—	—
no	soft yellow	D	3	perpetual	15'	O	C	—	—
le Brunner, imbing	pink	D	2	June/July	20'	O	C	F	—
plin's Pink Climber	pink	S-D	o	June/July	15'	O	C	—	—
se du Feu	scarlet	D	2	June/July	12'	O	C	—	—
ea's Golden Rambler	yellow	D	4	June/July	10'	O	C	—	—
gance	primrose	D	2	June	20'	O	C	—	—
ly Gray	buff yellow	D	3	June/July	15'	O	C	F	—
cité et Perpétue	blush	D	2	July	15'	O	C	—	—
bes Kiftsgate	cream	S	5	June/July	30'	O	C	—	—
land, The	blush	S-D	3	June/July	15'	O	C	—	—
re de Dijon	buff	D	4	perpetual	15'	O	C	—	—
den Showers	yellow	D	3	perpetual	10'	O	Sh C	F	—
dfinch	yellow	S-D	4	June/July	10'	O	C	—	—
del	blush, carmine	D	2	June/July	15'	O	C	—	—
rence Johnston	yellow	D	4	June/July	20'	O	C	—	—
giscuspis	white	S	5	August	20'	O	C	—	yes
e Alfred Carrière	white	D	4	perpetual	25'	O	C	—	—
;	apricot	S-D	3	June/July	15'	O	C	—	—
maid	yellow	S	2	perpetual	20'	O	C	F	—
Dawn, The	blush	D	4	perpetual	10'	O	C	—	—
's Himalayan Musk ambler	blush	D	5	July	40'	O	C	—	—
's Lemon Pillar	white	D	4	June/July†	15'	O	C	—	—
e	primrose	D	1	June/July	20'	O	C	F	—
bling Rector	white	S-D	5	July	20'	O	C	—	—
ona	crimson, pink	S	4	June	8'	O	C	—	—

ender † Unpredictable

| Group/Variety | Colour | Flowers | | Flowering period | Size | Habit | Uses | Foliage |
		Type	Scent					
Seven Sisters	mauve, mixed	S-D	1	July	30′	O	C	—
Vielchenblau	blue, mauve	S-D	2	June/July	15′	O	C	—
Wedding day	white	S	4	July	20′	O	C	—
Zéphirine Drouhin	cerise	D	4	perpetual	15′	O	Sh C H	—

A Further Selection – Brief Notes

I mentioned earlier that there were many shrub roses, other than those in my main selection. Here are brief details of quite a few more that you might like to try and that you may see in catalogues, though some of them may not be too easy to get hold of. All are worth their place in a collection.

SPECIES

Californica plena: Pink, semi-double. 6 × 5 ft. June/July. Scented.

Canina andersonii: Often listed simply as Andersonii. Pink, single. 6 × 8 ft. June/July. Scented. Heps.

Carolina plena: Shell-pink, double. 2 × 2 ft. July.

Cinnamomea plena: Pink, double. 4 × 3 ft. May/June. Scented.

Davidii: Pink, single. 9 × 8 ft. Late July. Scented. Heps.

Farreri persetosa: The Three-penny Bit Rose. Pink, single. 6 × 8 ft. Early June. Scented. Heps.

Fedtschenkoana: White, 1½–2 in., yellow stamens, single. 8 × 6 ft. Flowers all summer – unusual for a species. Young shoots and leaves purple-tinted. Mature leaves pale grey-green. Heps.

Foetida: Yellow, single. 5 × 4 ft. June/July. Scented.

Foliolosa: Pink, single. 4 × 3 ft. July/August. Scented. Autumn colour.

Hugonis: Pale yellow, single. 7 × 6 ft. May/June. Scented.

Macrantha Daisy Hill: Blush pink, semi-double. 5 × 9 ft. June/July. Scented. Heps.

Macrantha Düsterlohe: Pink, semi-double. 4 × 8 ft. June/July. Heps. Slight scent. Pillar or shrub.

Macrantha Raubritter: Pink, semi-double. 3 × 6 ft. June/July. Slight scent. A sprawler.

Macrophylla: Deep pink, single, large. 10 × 10 ft. June/July. Scented. Heps.

Moyesii Fred Streeter: Cerise-pink, single. 7 × 7 ft. June. Heps.

Moyesii Sealing Wax: Pink, single. 8 × 7 ft. June. Heps.

Moyesii Superba: Dusky crimson, semi-double. 7 × 6 ft. June. Compact for a Moyesii.

Nitida: Pink, single. 2 × 1 ft. June/July. Scented. Heps. Freely suckering. Crimson/scarlet autumn colour.

Paulii: White, single. 4 × 15 ft. June/July. Scented. Ground cover.

Primula: Yellow, single. 6 × 8 ft. May/June. Scented. Aromatic foliage.

Roxburghii: (The Burr Rose and The Chestnut Rose) Pale pink, shading to white eye, single. 6 × 4 ft. Late June/July. Grown more for its pinnate leaves with many leaflets, for its greyish, peeling bark, and for its curious prickly heps and calyx, which resemble small chestnuts, than for its flowers. The double form R. *roxburghii plena* is rather less vigorous.

Sericea Heather Muir: White, single. 9 × 9 ft. June/July. Scented. Heps.

Sericea Hidcote Gold: Yellow, single. 7 × 7 ft. May/June.

Setigera: Pink, single. 4 × 9 ft. August. Scented.

Setipoda: Pink, single. 8 × 8 ft. June/July. Scented. Heps. Fragrant foliage.

Spinosissima altaica: Cream, single. 6 × 5 ft. May.

Spinosissima bicolor: Pink, reverse paler, semi-double. 3 × 2 ft. May.

Spinosissima Double White: White, double (not unexpectedly). 5 × 4 ft. May. Scented.

Spinosissima Double Yellow: Yellow, double or semi-double. 5 × 4 ft. May. Slight scent.

Spinosissima lutea maxima: Yellow, single. 5 × 4 ft. May/June.

Note: All the *spinosissimas* above sucker freely.

Spinosissima Frühlingschnee: Cream, semi-double. 4 × 5 ft. Late May/June. Scented.

Spinosissima Frühlingszauber: Cerise and gold blend, semi-double. 5 × 3 ft. Late May/June. Scented. Heps.

Spinosissima Harisonii: Yellow, semi-double. 5 × 3 ft. May. Scented.

Virginiana: Cerise-pink, single. 4 × 9 ft. July/August. Scented. Heps. Brilliant autumn colour.

Virginiana plena: (Rose d'Amour). Pink, double. July/August. 6 × 6 ft. Faint scent.

Wardii culta: White with crimson centre, single. 6 × 6 ft. June/July. Faint scent.

Willmottiae: Mauvish-pink, single. 7 × 9 ft. June/July. Scented. Heps.

Xanthina: Yellow, double. 6 × 6 ft. May/June. Scented.

GALLICAS

Assemblage des Beautés: Crimson-scarlet, double. 4 × 3 ft. June/July.

Belle Isis: Pale salmon-pink, double. 3 × 3 ft. June/July.

Conditorum: Purplish-crimson, semi-double. Scented. 4 × 3 ft. June/July.

Cramoisi Picoté: Bright crimson, double. 4 × 3 ft. June/July.

Duc de Guiche: Crimson, shaded purple, double. 4 × 4 ft. June/July.

Duchesse d'Angoulême: Blush-pink, double. 3 × 3 ft. June/July.

Duchesse de Buccleugh: Magenta-pink, very double, quartered. 5 × 4 ft. June/July.

Duchesse de Montebello: Shell-pink, double. Scented. 4 × 3 ft. June/July.

Georges Vibert: Crimson and blush, striped and quartered. Double. 4 × 3 ft. June/July. Scented.

Gloire de France: Purplish mauve, fading to lilac at petal edges. 3 × 3 ft. June/July.

La Plus Belle des Ponctuées: Pink, dotted and splashed white, double. 6 × 4 ft. June/July.

Perle des Panachées: Striped white and crimson, semi-double. 3 × 2 ft. June/July.

President de Sèze: Maroon-crimson, lilac edged, double. 4 × 3 ft. June/July. Scented.

Tuscany: Maroon, semi-double. 4 × 3 ft. June/July.

DAMASKS

Hebe's Lip: Cream, sometimes edged crimson. 4 × 3 ft. Semi-double. June/July. Scented.

Ispahan: Blush-pink, double. 7 × 5 ft. June/July. Scented.

Kazanlik: Rose-pink, paler reverse, double. 6 × 5 ft. June/July. Scented – source of Attar of Roses.

Léda: (The Painted Damask) White, edged crimson, double. 3 × 3 ft. June/July. Scented.

Marie Louise: Pink, double. 4 × 3 ft. June/July. Scented.

Omar Khayyam: Pink, double, quartered. 3 × 2 ft. June/July. Originally from seed from a rose on Omar Khayyam's grave. Not distinguished otherwise. Scented.

Rose d'Hiver: Shell-pink, fading at edges, double. 4 × 3 ft. June/July.

ALBAS

Blush Hip: Soft pink, double. 10 × 7 ft. June/July. Can be grown on pillar.

Mme Legras de St Germain: White with primrose centre, double. 6 × 6 ft. June/July.

CENTIFOLIAS

Bullata: Pink, double. 4 × 4 ft. June/July. Distinctive, crinkled foliage.

Juno: Blush-white, double. 4 × 4 ft. June/July.

Paul Ricault: Rich pink, double, quartered. 4 × 3 ft. June/July.

Reine des Centfeuilles: Pink, double, quartered. 4 × 3 ft. June/July.

Spong: Pink, double. 4 × 3 ft. June/July.

The Bishop: Cerise-purple, fading lilac-grey, lilac reverse, double. 5 × 3 ft. June/July.

Unique Blanche: (White Provence). White, double. 4 × 4 ft. Late June/July. Scented.

MOSS ROSES

Baron de Wassanaer: Crimson, double. 5 × 3 ft. June/July. Scent. Moss rather scanty.

Blanche Moreau: Creamy-white, double. 6 × 4 ft. Recurrent. Brown moss. Can be grown on pillar. Scent.

Common Moss: Pink, double. 4 × 4 ft. June/July.

Comtesse de Murinais: White, double, quartered. 6 × 4 ft. June/July. Pillar or shrub. Scent.

Crimson Moss: Purplish-crimson, semi-double. 5 × 4 ft. June/July. Included as it appears in catalogues, but it is not good at opening its flowers except in the hottest summers.

Deuil de Paul Fontaine: Darkest crimson, double. 3 × 3 ft. Recurrent.

James Mitchell: Pink, small and double. 5 × 5 ft. Early June/July.

Jeanne de Montfort: Cerise-pink, double. 6 × 5 ft. Recurrent. Dark moss. Shrub or pillar. Scent.

Little Gem: Crimson, double. 4 × 2 ft. June/July. Scent.

Louis Gimard: Lilac-crimson blends, double. 5 × 3 ft. June/July.

Mme Delaroche-Lambert: Crimson-purple, double. 4 × 4 ft. Recurrent.

Mme Louis Lévêque: Pink, double. 5 × 3 ft. Recurrent. Scent.

Maréchal Davoust: Fuchsia-pink with lighter reverse, double. 4 × 4 ft. June/July.

Monsieur Péllison: Pink, double. 4 × 4 ft. June/July. Brown moss.

Park Jewel: Strong pink, double. 4 × 6 ft. June/July. Shrub or pillar. Scent.

Shailer's White Moss: (White Bath). White, double. 4 × 3 ft. June/July.

Striped Moss: (Oeuillet Panachée). Pale pink, striped carmine, double. 4 × 3 ft. June/July.

PORTLAND ROSES

Mabel Morrison: Pink, fading white, double. 4 × 2 ft. Perpetual.

The Portland Rose: Crimson, semi-double. 2 × 2 ft. Recurrent. Historical interest.

CHINA ROSES

Cramoisi Supérieur: Dark crimson, semi-double. 3 × 2 ft. Perpetual.

Jenny Wren: Salmon, paler at edges. Scented. Double. 4 × 2 ft. Perpetual.

Fellemberg: Deep pink, double. 8 × 6 ft. Perpetual. Pillar.

Hermosa: Lilac-pink, double. 3 × 2 ft. Recurrent. Scented.

Old Blush: Pink, semi-double. 4 × 3 ft. Perpetual. Faint scent.

BOURBONS AND HYBRID PERPETUALS

Baron Girod de l'Ain: (HP) Crimson, edged white, double. 5 × 4 ft. Recurrent. Scented.

Baronne Prévost: (HP) Pink, double, quartered. 5 × 3 ft. Perpetual Scented.

Bourbon Queen: (B) Magenta-pink, double. 6 × 5 ft. June/July. Scented.

Champion of the World: (B) Pink, double. 5 × 3 ft. Perpetual. Scented.

Eugène Fürst: (HP) Crimson with lighter reverse, double. 5 × 3 ft. Recurrent. Scented.

Fisher Holmes: (HP) Dark crimson, double. 5 × 3 ft. Recurrent. Scented.

Gruss an Teplitz: (Early HT) Crimson, double. 6 × 5 ft. Perpetual. Scented. 15 ft. as wall climber.

Mme Lauriol de Barny: (B) Pink, double. 6 × 5 ft. June/July. Scented. Pillar, or shrub.

Paul Neyron: (HP) Deep pink, double. 6 × 3 ft. Recurrent. Little scent. Shrub or pillar.

Rose du Roi à Fleurs Pourpres: (B) Purplish crimson, double. 3 × 2 ft. June/July. Scented.

Souvenir d'Alphonse Lavallée: (HP) Dark crimson, double. 7 × 4 ft. Recurrent. Scented. Shrub or pillar.

Souvenir du Docteur Jamain: (HP) Maroon-purple, double. 6 ×

3 ft. (10 ft. on a wall.) Recurrent. Scented. Requires good soil.
Vick's Caprice: (HP) Pink, splashed white, double. 3 × 2 ft. Perpetual. Scented.

RUGOSAS

Dr Eckener: Yellow, flushed pink, double. 9 × 8 ft. Recurrent. Scented.
Grootendorst Supreme: Dark crimson, double, frilled edges. 5 × 4 ft. Perpetual. F. J. Grootendorst sport.
Hansa: Crimson-purple, double. 5 × 5 ft. Perpetual. Scented.
Mrs Anthony Waterer: Crimson, double. 5 × 6 ft. Half-heartedly recurrent.
Schneelicht: White, single. 5 × 8 ft. June/July. Scented.

HYBRID MUSKS

Daphne: Pink, semi-double. 5 × 4 ft. Perpetual. Scented.
Morgensonne: Golden-yellow, double. 5 × 5 ft. Perpetual. Scented.
Trier: Blush-white, semi-double. 7 × 6 ft. Recurrent. Scented. The ancestor of all the Hybrid Musks.

MODERN SHRUB ROSES

Cerise Bouquet: Cerise-crimson, semi-double. 6 × 6 ft. June/July. Scented.
Kathleen Ferrier: Salmon-pink, semi-double. 5 × 4 ft. Perpetual. A floribunda. Scented.
Lady Sonia: Yellow, semi-double. 5 × 3 ft. Recurrent.
Lichterloh: Scarlet, semi-double. 4 × 2 ft. Perpetual. Scented. A floribunda.
Märchenland: Salmon-pink, semi-double. 4 × 4 ft. Perpetual. A floribunda. Scented.
Norwich Gold: Salmon with deep yellow reverse, double. 5 × 3 ft. Perpetual. A floribunda. Scented.
Reveil Dijonnais: Cerise with yellow centres, single. 8 × 6 ft. Bush or climber. Recurrent. Scented.

Till Eulenspiegel: Crimson with white eye, single. 4 × 8 ft. June/ July. Faint scent.

CLIMBERS AND RAMBLERS
(A mixture of old and new)

Allen Chandler: (C – HT or HP) Scarlet-crimson, large, semi-double. 15-20 ft. Early and recurrent. Slight scent.

Banksiae alba plena: (C) Small white, double. 25 ft. May. Scented. Warm walls only.

Blairi No. 2: (C) Cerise-pink, double. 18 ft. June/July. Scented.

Bracteata: (The Macartney Rose) (C) White, single. 20 ft. Perpetual. Scented.

Breeze Hill: (R) Cream-apricot, fading cream-white, double. 12 ft. June/July. Scented. Can be grown as a shrub.

Copenhagen: (C – HT) Scarlet, large, double. 8 ft. Scented. Recurrent. Pillar or wall. Coppery leaves. An offspring of Ena Harkness.

Crimson Conquest: (R) Velvety scarlet-crimson, small, semi-double. 15 ft. June/July. Slight scent. Rampant.

Crimson Shower: (R) Crimson, small, semi-double, pompons. 15 ft. Slight scent. Good for weeping standard. Like, but much better than, the often listed Excelsa, but late flowering in August/September, when few other climbers are in full display.

Deprez à Fleur Jaune: (C) Peach-yellow, double. 18 ft. June/July. Perpetual. Scented. Tender.

Dr W. Van Fleet: (R) Pale flesh-pink, double, large for a rambler and in large trusses. 15 ft. June/July. Scented. Very free.

Etude: (C) Deep rose-pink in clusters, semi-double. 10 ft. Scented. Free, recurrent bloom. Wall or pillar.

Fortune's Yellow: (R) Flame-orange, semi-double. 18 ft. June/ July. Scented. Tender.

François Juranville: (R) Salmon-pink. 25 ft. June/July. Scented.

Gerbe Rose: (R) Pink, double and quartered. 10 ft. Recurrent. Scented. A pillar rose.

Grandmère Jenny, Climbing: (C – HT) Apricot, edged and suffused pink, large and loosely double. 10 ft. June/July. Slight scent. Pillar.

Guinée: (C – HT) Deep, dusky red with scarlet tones, large, double. 18 ft. Very fragrant. Recurrent.

Hamburger Phoenix: (C) Deep red, cupped, semi-double. 9 ft. Recurrent. Little scent. Dark, glossy leaves. Pillar or shrub.

Jersey Beauty: (R) Buff, fading cream, single. 18 ft. June/July. Scented.

Kew Rambler: (R) Pink with white eye, single. 15 ft. Scented. June/July. Orange heps.

Lady Hillingdon, Climbing: (C – HT) Apricot-yellow, double. 20 ft. Perpetual. Scented. Tender.

Le Rève: (C) Yellow, semi-double. 15 ft. June/July. Scented.

Leverkussen: (C) Golden yellow, large, semi-double. 10-12 ft. Perpetual. Pillar or shrub, Scented. June/July.

Mme Caroline Testout, Climbing: (C – HT) Soft pink, sometimes edged carmine, large, globular, double. 20 ft. Recurrent, the second crop often better than the first. Fragrant.

Mme Grégoire Staechelin: (C – HT) Pink, double. 30 ft. Late May/June. Very free. Scented.

Maréchal Niel: (C) Pale yellow, double. 15 ft. Recurrent. Scented. Very tender.

Multiflora: (R) Small white, double. 12 ft. June/July. Scented. Can be used as a shrub.

Parkdirektor Riggers: (C) Velvety-crimson, large, semi-double in large clusters. 15 ft. Recurrent if heps removed. Very healthy and one of the best reds. Wall or pillar.

Pink Perpetué: (C) Bright rose-pink, deeper reverse, double in clusters. 10 ft. Scented. Recurrent and very free. Wall or pillar.

Raymond Chenault: (C) Glowing scarlet, large, semi-double. 8 ft. June/July. Fragrant. Pillar or shrub.

Rêve d'Or: (R) Buff-yellow, double. 14 ft. Perpetual. Scented.

Rose-Marie Viaud: (R) Magenta-pink, double. 15 ft. Late June/July. No thorns. Shrub or climber.

Soldier Boy: (C) Scarlet, single, large. 10 ft. Early and then Intermittent. Good glossy leaves. Pillar or shrub.

Sombreuil: (C – HT) White, shading to pink in the centre, double, opening flat. 15 ft. Scented. Perpetual and best on a warm wall.

Souvenir de Claudius Denoyel: (C – HT) Crimson, double. 20 ft. Recurrent. Scented.

Spectabilis: (R) Lilac-pink, double. 7 ft. June/July. Light scent. A pillar rose or shrub.

Sweet Sultan: (C – HT) Crimson, shading maroon, large, single. 8 ft. Scented, recurrent. Pillar or shrub.

Violette: (R) Dark crimson, double. 15 ft. June/July. Light scent.

Wichuraiana: (R) White, single. 20 ft. July/August. Scented. Will sprawl naturally for ground-cover. Parent of a whole family of ramblers.

William Allen Richardson: (C) Orange-yellow, fading white, double. 12 ft. Recurrent. Scented. Tender.

Bibliography

ALL the books, except those starred, are in the author's collection. Some deal exclusively with the old roses and some only have sections on them. Which is which can, in most cases, be gathered from the titles or the date of publication. Some have long been out of print and can only be obtained second-hand, or be seen in libraries. Some are really only for the dedicated enthusiast. Look, and in the case of the rarer ones, approach your bank for a loan, before you buy.

American Rose Society Annuals – various (USA).
*Bunyard, A. E. *Old Garden Roses*, Collingridge, 1936.
Coates, P. *Flowers in History*, Weidenfeld and Nicolson, 1970.
Fairbrother, F. *Roses*, Penguin, 1958.
Fletcher, H. L. V. (Compiler). *The Rose Anthology*, Newnes 1963.
Foster Mellier, Rev. *The Book of the Rose*, Macmillan 1864.
Gault, S. M. and Synge, P. M. *The Dictionary of Roses in Colour*, Ebury Press and Michael Joseph, 1970.
Gerard, J. *Gerard's Herball* (Abridged from the 1599 original in 1927), Spring Books, 1964.
Henslow, T. G. W. *The Rose Encyclopedia*, C. Arthur Pearson, 1922.
Hole, S. Reynolds. *A Book About Roses*, William Blackwood, 1869.
Jekyll, G. and Mawley, E. *Roses for English Gardens*, Country Life, 1902.
Kiaer, E. and Hancke, V. *Methuen Handbook of Roses*, Methuen, 1966.
Kordes, W. *Roses*, Studio, 1964.
Le Grice, E. B. *Rose Growing Complete*, Faber and Faber, 1965.
Mansfield, T. C. *Roses in Colour and Cultivation*, Collins, 1947.
McFarland, J. H. Company, Modern Roses VI, 1965 (USA).
McFarland, J. H. *Roses of the World in Colour*, Houghton Mifflin, 1936 (USA).
Park, B. *Collins Guide to Roses*, Collins, 1956.
Park, B. *The World of Roses*, Harrap, 1962.
Paul, W. *The Rose Garden*, Kent and Co., 1848.

*Pemberton, Rev. J. H. *Roses – Their History, Development and Cultivation,* 1908.

Poulsen, S. *Poulsen on the Rose,* MacGibbon and Kee, 1955.

*Redouté, P. J. *Les Roses,* Didot, 1817–1824 (France).

Redouté, P. J. *Roses (A Selection),* The Ariel Press, 1954.

Redouté, P. J. *Roses 2 (A Selection),* The Ariel Press, 1956.

*Rivers, T. *The Rose Amateur's Guide,* Longmans Green, 1837.

Rose, The. Various issues.

Royal Horticultural Society's Journal, various issues.

Royal National Rose Society's Annuals, various.

Sanders, T. W. (Ed.). *Cultivated Roses,* Collingridge, 1899.

*Sitwell, S. and Russell, J. *Old Garden Roses* (2 vols) 1955–1957.

Steen, N. *The Charm of Old Roses,* Herbert Jenkins, 1966.

Thomas, H. H. *The Rose Book,* Cassell, 1913.

Thomas, G. S. *Climbing Roses Old and New,* Phoenix House, 1965.

Thomas G. S. *Manual of Shrub Roses, The,* Sunningdale Nurseries, 1964.

Thomas, G. S. *Old Shrub Roses, The,* Phoenix House, 1957.

Thomas, G. S. *Shrub Roses of Today,* Phoenix House, 1962.

*Wilmot, E. *The Genus Rosa,* John Murray, 1914.

All rose-lovers should join the Royal National Rose Society. The subscription is only £1.75. Write to The Secretary, Chiswell Green Lane, St Albans, Herts, to see what incredible value you get for your money.

General Index

Index of Roses

Numbers in **bold** type refer to principal entries